CW01655499

Uniforms and Insignia of the Royal Armoured Corps since 1946

John Bodsworth

MLRS
2006

Printed and published by
Military Library Research Service Ltd
2006

ISBN
978-1-905973-53-8

CONTENTS

INTRODUCTION

The study of British military uniforms is not the exact science that many collectors, historians and researchers would wish. Rather, it is the story of continual change, brought about by a whole variety of factors, of which the following are in no specific order.

The time taken to design new uniforms and accoutrements, possibly with trials, can take over ten years, in some instances. The issue of these to a large army, spread worldwide, with major cost implications, can in some instances take a further ten years. Once issued, many items are further modified to correct deficiencies not envisaged previously.

In the 1950s, large amounts for stock were kept ready for war. This situation has now changed, with much smaller stocks available, giving greater flexibility for change. In an ever-changing world, this avoids having large amounts of redundant stock in storage. The downside being any problems in manufacture, or distribution, can lead to shortages.

Cost, whether to the War Office, or the individual, can mean that uniforms and accoutrements usually continue to be worn whilst serviceable, possibly for twenty, or more, years.

Other changes, affecting uniform, include new tactics, weapons and personal protection, e.g. body armour, Nuclear, Biological and Chemical kit, etc. New materials, such as breathable, waterproof clothing and flame-retardant clothing, have also brought about changes, especially in clothing for hot and cold climates. Changes in fashion also influence the design of new uniforms.

After all of this has been achieved, the uniform is then decorated with a whole variety of insignia, showing regimental distinctions, rank, proficiency and trade skills. No regiment or battalion, wants to look identical to another, hence there are always minor differences between them. The CO and the RSM also have some input to what is worn and how, within their unit. Finally, if it is at all possible to wear something the wrong way, then it probably has been.

Since 1945, the uniforms worn by the British Army have seen considerable change. All that can be said is that they look similar although, on closer inspection, this is usually not the case. Illustrated here is a selection of the various orders of dress worn by the Royal Armoured Corps, in an attempt to show some of this rich tapestry of history in wear.

The Royal Armoured Corps was formed in April 1939, from the Royal Tank Regiment and the Cavalry Regiments of the Line. The RAC itself is an administrative and training body only, its badges and uniforms only being worn by staff and recruits.

The Household Cavalry are in a unique position: whilst trained as an armoured reconnaissance regiment, they also perform ceremonial duties with the Household Division. As all of their Full Dress uniforms and accoutrements are catalogued separately, in Clothing Regulations and Dress Regulations, details of these will hopefully be covered in other publications on the Household Division. The 1st Royal Dragoons have been included here, as they were a cavalry regiment up until 1969, when they were amalgamated with the Royal Horse Guards, and became part of the Household Division. In the Order of Precedence flow chart, those regiments highlighted in purple are part of the Household Division, details of which are excluded.

During the Second World War, six new cavalry regiments were raised. The 22nd Dragoons, 23rd Hussars, 24th Lancers and 27th Lancers were all formed in December 1940. The 25th Dragoons and 26th Hussars were raised in India, in February 1941. The 24th Lancers and the 26th Hussars were both disbanded during the war. However, the four remaining regiments existed until June 1948, and as such are worth a mention. However, their orders of dress were limited, battledress in the main and Service Dress for officers. In addition, few could have been issued with Pattern 1946 battledress, let alone 1947 Pattern battledress. They are therefore not included here, though details of these may be found in *British Army Uniforms and Insignia of World War Two*, written by Brian L. Davis.

In 1946, the Royal Armoured Corps consisted of 20 Cavalry of the Line regiments (excluding the Household Cavalry) and 8 separate Royal Tank Regiments. In 2006, after various amalgamations, there are only 8 cavalry regiments and 2 Royal Tank Regiments. The Order of Precedence flow chart shows these changes, the dates give the formation of the new regiment after amalgamation. Those regiments highlighted in yellow are still in existence. Sadly, those in blue, or green, no longer exist.

ACKNOWLEDGEMENTS

I am greatly indebted to the following for their continuing help and support in this project. Rog Dennis, David Linaker and Jim MacDonald.

Also to Home Headquarters, The Light Dragoons, Newcastle. Roberta Twinn at The Light Dragoons (15th/19th King's Royal Hussars) Museum Collection, Discovery Museum, Newcastle and Hand & Lock, London.

Finally to the many interesting people I met during this project, who either answered, or attempted to answer, my many odd and strange questions.

ORDERS OF DRESS

No. 1 Dress – Temperate ceremonial dress. This was first worn at the 1937 Coronation of King George VI. Interrupted by the Second World War, an improved version began to be issued in 1947. Intended for the whole army, cost implications restricted it mainly to Officers and NCOs. The Royal Armoured Corps (excluding the Royal Tank Regiment) wear shoulder chains on No.1 Dress, instead of shoulder straps. These originated, after the Indian Mutiny, in the 2nd Punjab Cavalry, where one officer later sewed curb chains on his shoulders to ward off sword cuts. Sam Browne, a fellow officer in the regiment, had lost his left arm to a mutineer's sword, in an action that earned him the Victoria Cross. This uniform still continues to be worn, usually as a pooled item, for special ceremonial occasions and weddings.

No.2 Dress – Temperate parade uniform (Service Dress). The Officers' pattern has changed only slightly since 1912. The cavalry pattern evolved differently the standard pattern. Firstly, the box pleated breast pockets and box side pockets were superseded by plain patch breast pockets and *jetted* side pockets. Secondly, some regiments changed to a khaki cavalry twill material, instead of the more usual khaki barathea material. With the reduction in the number of cavalry regiments, attempts have been made over the years, to standardise officers' Service Dress. They have met only with limited success, as many regiments have retained their traditions in regard to their dress distinctions. Thus variations in pockets, pocket flaps, material and colour, as well as a vast array of regimental embellishments, are still encountered today.

Other Ranks began to be issued with No.2 Dress in 1961. The early patterns are easily identified by their box pleated breast pockets. A new pattern was introduced in 1980, in a lighter weight material and again easily identified by its breast pockets, which are of the plain patch type.

No.3 Dress – Warm weather ceremonial uniform. This is the tropical version of No.1 Dress, in white drill material. All badges and embellishments are similar to those worn on No.1 Dress.

No.4 Dress – Warm weather Service Dress. This is the tropical version of Service Dress, it is worn exclusively by Officers. It was originally made from gabardine, later changing to a polyester and wool weave in the 1970s.

No.5 Dress – Battledress. This was originally adopted just before the Second World War, with a number of official patterns being issued. Some officers also purchased a superior quality of battledress from their tailor, especially when serving overseas. This order of dress was phased out in the 1970s, the number remaining redundant until 1990.

No.5 Dress – Desert combat dress. This order of dress came into existence during the Gulf War of 1990. Since then the pattern has not only changed, but a number of other items have been added to it.

No.6 Dress – Tropical Dress. This was originally the equivalent of battledress for tropical and semi-tropical areas. It was made from either Khaki Drill material, or Olive Green material, dependant on local vegetation. As the cost of materials and labour in the Middle East and Far East was very cheap, most Officers and some NCOs bought locally made uniforms either in light khaki, or olive green.

No.6 Dress – Warm weather parade uniform (Bush Jacket). With the demise of BD, KD and OG, a newer form of uniform was adopted. This consists of a lightweight, stone coloured jacket and trousers. During the 1980s both the pattern and material for this was changed.

No.7 Dress – Warm weather barrack dress. This consists of a lightweight, stone coloured, short sleeved shirt and trousers, the latter designed to be worn with the appropriate dress, or working belt.

No.8 Dress – Mess Dress (Tropical) This later became No.11 Dress.

No.8 Dress – Temperate combat dress. Consisting originally of a green sateen combat uniform, this changed to temperate Disruptive Pattern Material (DPM) in 1968. Since then a number of patterns have been worn.

Body armour – The Daily Telegraph reported in 1958, that body armour was being used by British Troops, on peace-keeping duties in Cyprus. These are listed in the 1960 Catalogue of Clothing and Necessaries, as being the US M 1952A pattern. This has now become part of the soldier's combat dress, when employed on internal security, peace-keeping and active service. The Royal Armoured Corps has been employed on all of these. Originally green in colour, various patterns have evolved over the years, with temperate DPM, Desert DPM and United Nations blue covers. Only one example has been included in this book, as space precludes a more detailed study.

NBC – Nuclear, Biological and Chemical warfare became a much greater threat during the post-war period. During the early 1960s, a new respirator was introduced, followed shortly afterwards by the first NBC suit. The early NBC suits were greyish in colour, later replaced by improved versions in green, DPM and ultimately Desert DPM. While all soldiers are trained in NBC warfare, the only operational use of them was in the first Gulf War of 1990-91. Only one example is included here, as space precludes a more detailed study of this specialist subject.

No.9 Dress – Tropical combat dress. This consists of a lightweight DPM uniform.

No.10 Dress – Temperate Mess Dress. Officers have worn these ever since Victorian times. The wearing of Mess Dress, by WOs and NCOs, only goes back to the 1960s. These were usually based on the officers' patterns, but less ornate, in an attempt to make them affordable.

No.11 Dress – Warm weather Mess Dress. This usually consists of a white, lightweight version of No. 10 Dress. Again, WOs and NCOs adopting it much later than Officers.

No.12 Dress – Protective clothing For the RAC this order of dress consists of coveralls, essential for working on vehicles.

No.13 Dress – Temperate barrack dress Pullover, shirt and trousers. Officers of many regiments, have adopted a special pattern and colour of regimental pullover. Again, in many regiments, Senior NCOs and WOs have also adopted a special pattern of regimental pullover, based on the officers' pattern. Junior ranks wear the issue pullover, or jersey, some of which are fitted with regimental embellishments.

No.14 Dress – Shirt Sleeve Order – This consists of trousers, worn with the appropriate dress, or working belt. The shirt is worn with the top button open and the sleeves rolled up to one inch above the elbow.

Full Dress – This was worn by all of the army until the outbreak of war in 1914. After the war, it was restricted to the Household Division (Household Cavalry and Foot Guards). However, a few cavalry regiments retain a small number of these for special ceremonial duties.

Band dress – This is usually based on an extra embellished version of No.1 Dress, or on Full Dress.

Blue patrols – This was originally a less ornate version of No.1 Dress. They were worn up until the introduction of No.1 Dress. Some continued to wear them out, in place of No.1 Dress, whilst others had them converted to No.1 Dress. Some regiments and units still refer to No.1 Dress as blue patrols, although this is not strictly correct. For most of the army, blue patrols became obsolete with the introduction of No.1 Dress. However, the Scottish infantry regiments still retain these in their original form. They usually wear them in the Mess, where they are considered as being smart and a more comfortable alternative to No.1 Dress, or Mess Dress. In the new Royal Regiment of Scotland this is designated No.15 Dress – Blue patrols.

ORDER OF PRECEDENCE FLOW CHART

In the following flow-charts it may be noted that two numbers are absent. The original 19th C. Light Dragoon regiments provided the inter-mixed series of Dragoons, Hussars and lancers. Despite the 1922 amalgamations, in 1945 there were still a relatively complete sequence of Dragoon Guards and Dragoons/Hussars/Lancers, with the exception of 6th DG and 6th Dragoons. In 1922, 3rd DG amalgamated with 6th DG, becoming 3rd DG. Instead of combining their numbers, both elements of their respective titles were joined, "PoW" (from 3rd DG) and "Carabiniers" (from 6th DG). At the same time, 5th (Princess Charlotte of Wales's) DG were amalgamated with 6th (Iniskilling) Dragoons. Thus the odd Dragoon regiment, aside from 1st (Royal) Dragoons and 2nd Dragoons (RSG) disappeared.

ORDER OF PRECEDENCE

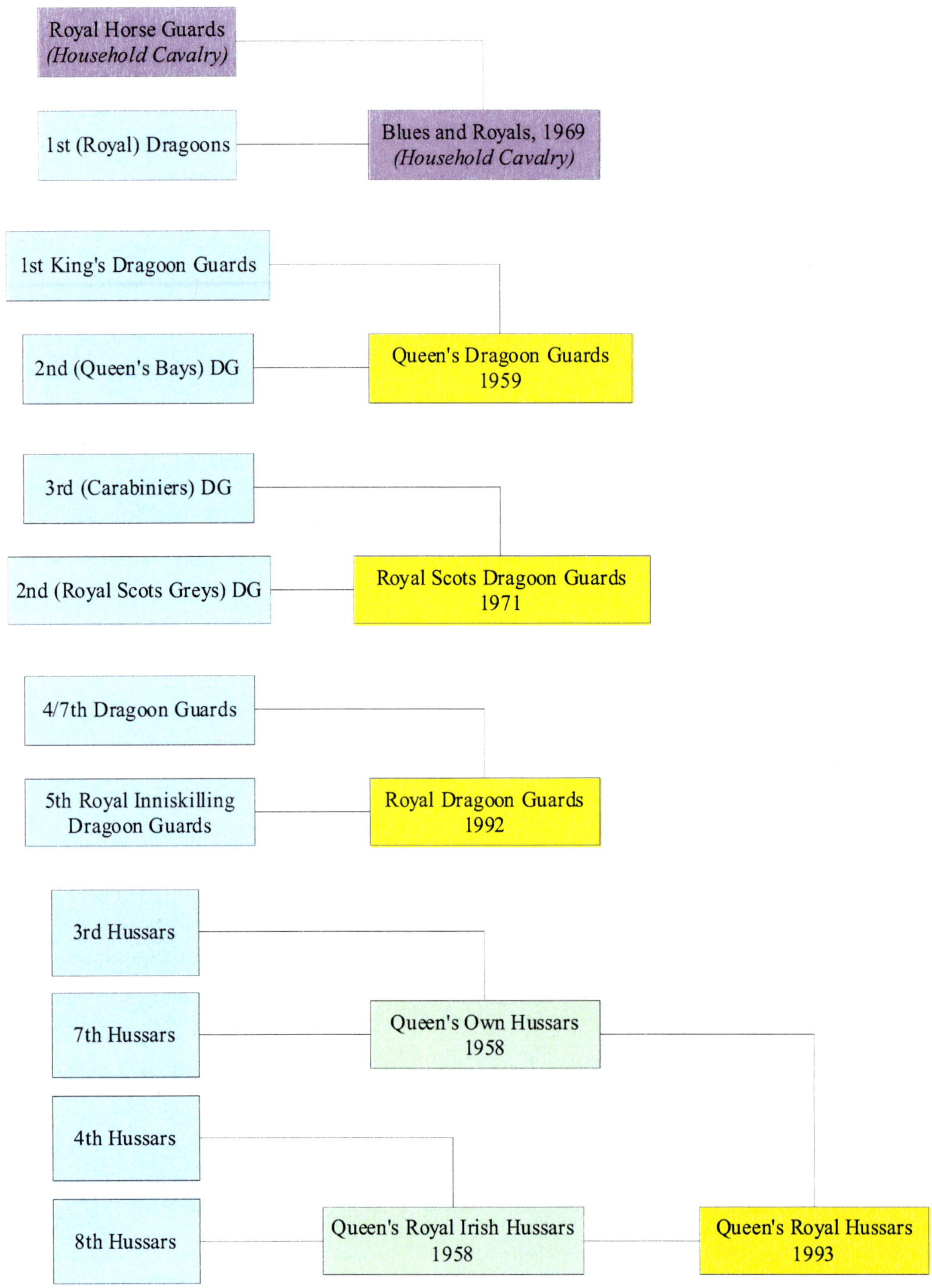

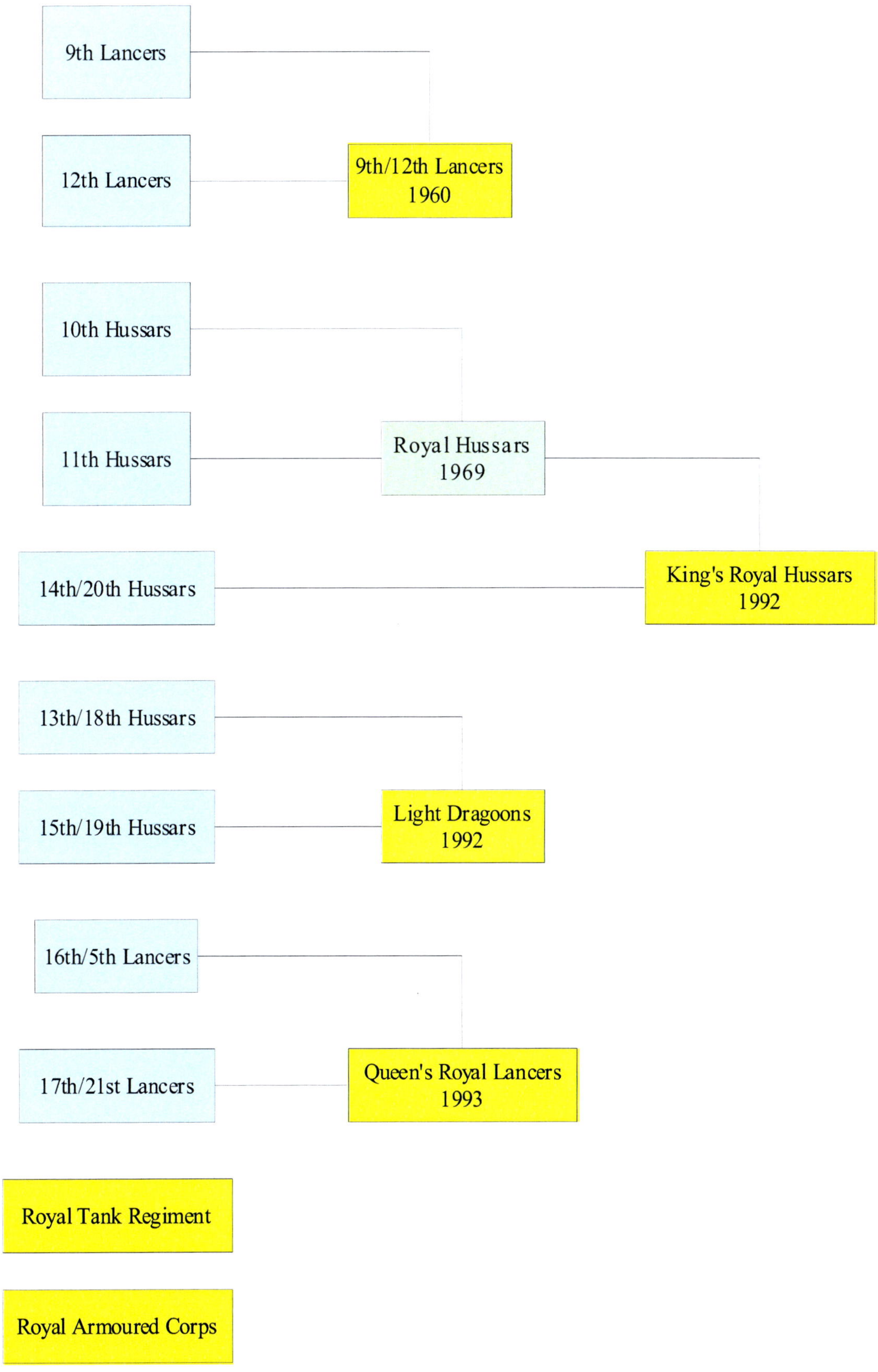
9th Lancers
12th Lancers
9th/12th Lancers 1960
10th Hussars
11th Hussars
Royal Hussars 1969
14th/20th Hussars
King's Royal Hussars 1992
13th/18th Hussars
15th/19th Hussars
Light Dragoons 1992
16th/5th Lancers
17th/21st Lancers
Queen's Royal Lancers 1993
Royal Tank Regiment
Royal Armoured Corps

3rd CARABINIERS

No.1 Dress

Forage Cap – Other Ranks wore a blue cap, with a yellow band and welt around the crown. All Officers used a similar cap, but with ¾-in gold *passing* on the peak.

Jacket – Blue, with shoulder chains. All Ranks wore collar badges. Chevrons and WOs badges were gold on yellow. NCOs also had an embroidered regimental arm badge. The Officers' jacket had plain patch breast pockets, with three-point flaps, which fastened with a concealed button. The side pockets were also of the plain patch type, with a flap similar to that on the breast pockets, but without a button. The sleeves were plain, without cuffs or buttons. Officers wore small rank badges, gilt without enamel.

Trousers – All Ranks wore blue trousers, with double white stripes, each ¾-in wide and $^{1}/_{8}$-in apart.

No.2 Dress

Fig.1a Officer wearing Service Dress, made from a light khaki barathea cloth. The plain patch breast pockets have rounded flaps. The plain patch side pockets have rectangular flaps and fasten with a small button. **Fig.1b** Shoulder strap, showing the plain polished brass rank star, which is $^{3}/_{5}$-inch wide. A special pattern of pig-skin Sam Browne belt was worn, supplied by Messrs Wilkinson, London. **Fig.1c** Shows the cross strap, which is fitted with 'Dog Lead' fastenings for attachment to the belt. The end with the stud adjustment, on the left, is attached to the front of the belt. The end with the buckle, on the right, is attached to the rear of the belt.

No.4 Dress – Warm weather service dress.

Fig.2a Shows the uniform worn by Major JDS Henderson. This, for the main part, follows 3rd Carabiniers officers' pattern of Service Dress, with plain patch breast pockets, with rounded flaps. However, they and a few other cavalry regiments adopted the practice of wearing shoulder chains on No.4 Dress. **Fig.2b** Shoulder chain. **Fig.2c** Trousers, made similarly to Service Dress trousers, complete with turn ups.

Fig.3a Cap badge. **Fig.3b** Collar badge. **Fig.3c** Gilding metal shoulder title, worn by All Ranks on Battledress. **Fig.3d** Gold anodised shoulder title, worn by Other Ranks in No.2 Dress. **Fig.3e** NCOs' arm badge, though other versions of this also exist. **3f** Embroidered version of NCOs' arm badge, worn on No.1 Dress.

Fig.4a Trooper, in the late 1960s, wearing the No.1 Mk., NBC Suit. Later versions had the hood attached as part of the smock. **Fig.4b** S6 respirator, this example made in 1963. **Fig.4c** White cotton inner gloves and black outer NBC gloves. To give full protection, black rubber overboots were also worn.

Fig.5 Shows the special regimental pattern of greatcoat worn by a Lt-Colonel. While the style follows the standard army officers' pattern, it differs in the following respects; leather buttons, yellow piping to the shoulder straps, collar and cuffs and cloth rank badges, embroidered on a yellow background.

Fig.6 Stable belt, this is worn with the buckles on the left side of the wearer, with the straps pointing to the rear. The two ornamental diagonal leather pieces fall on the right side of the wearer, these are designed to counteract the buckles on the left side.

3rd CARABINIERS

Fig.1a

Fig.1b

Fig.1c

Fig.2a

Fig.2b

Fig.2c

Fig.3a

Fig.3c

Fig.3d

Fig.3d

Fig.3e

Fig.3f

Fig.4a

Fig.4b

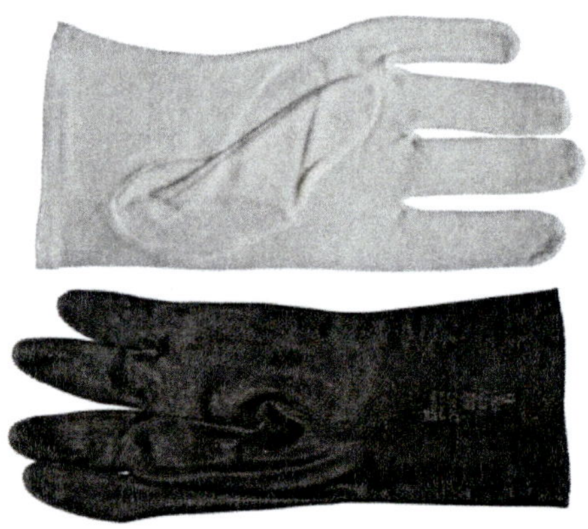

Fig.4c

Fig.5

Fig.6

4th/7th ROYAL DRAGOON GUARDS

No.1 Dress

Forage Cap – Other Ranks wear a blue cap, with a Royal Blue band and welt around the crown. All Officers used a similar cap, but with ¾-in gold *passing* on the peak.
Jacket – Blue, with shoulder chains. All Ranks had collar badges. Chevrons and WOs badges are of gold, on Royal Blue. NCOs also had a metal regimental arm badge. Officers wore standard rank badges.
Trousers – All Ranks wore blue trousers, with a single 1¾ in. wide yellow stripe.

No.2 Dress

Fig.1a Illustrates a Sergeant in 1964 Pattern No.2 Dress. He is wearing anodised collar badges, a white lanyard around his right arm and the medal ribbon for UN Cyprus medal. **Fig.1b** Shows the insignia on his right arm. On the shoulder strap are 4/7 RDG shoulder titles, while above his rank chevrons is his metal NCO's arm badge, worn on a black backing. **Fig.1c** In addition to the shoulder titles and rank badges, he has the regimental arm badge. This originated from a helmet flash, worn by the regiment during the Second World War.

No.2 Dress – Service Dress

Fig.3a shows the uniform worn by Major IS McGregor, originally made for him in 1963. It is made from whipcord, in a cavalry type pattern, with the box pleated breast pockets having rounded, triangular pointed flaps and inset side pockets. He has the ribbons for the War Medal 1939-45, General Service Medal, Campaign Service Medal and the 1953 Coronation Medal. The cuffs are plain, fastened by two buttons. Officers did not wear either lanyards, or the flash on their Service Dress uniforms. **Fig.3b** Shows the silver collar badge used by Officers. **Fig.3c** Illustrates the anodised rank and shoulder titles for this uniform. **Fig.3d** Shows the inside of this belt, clearly marked to the RSM, 4/7 DG. This is a special regimental pattern of Sam Browne with a whistle attached to the shoulder belt, which in turn has non-standard fittings.

No.10 Dress – Temperate Mess Dress

Other Ranks – 1939 Pattern jacket, scarlet with Royal Blue roll collar and cuffs and without shoulder straps. The front is fastened with two small linked regimental buttons. Rank badges are similar to those on No.1 Dress and NCOs wore a silver embroidered regimental arm badge. This jacket was worn with No.1 Dress trousers and a Royal Blue art silk cummerbund.
Officers – 1902 Pattern jacket, similar in colour to that worn by the Other Ranks, but much more ornate and with a stand collar.

Other Items of Dress

Fig.2 Shows a senior NCO's beret with badge. Corporals and below wore the cap badge, with a maroon backing on the issue blue beret. However, sergeants and above wore a collar badge, on a maroon backing, on their berets.

Stable belt – (from top to bottom) crimson 1¼ inches, yellow ½ inch and black 1¼ inches. The belt was fastened with two nickel plated single pronged, roller buckles and tan leather straps.

Side hat – Scarlet body, piped gold, with a dark blue tip. The flaps are dark blue, piped gold. No buttons were worn on this hat. Officers use a wire embroidered badge, on a dark blue backing. The Other Ranks side cap has cloth piping and was worn with a metal badge.

4th/7th ROYAL DRAGOON GUARDS

Fig.1a

Fig.2

Fig.1b

Fig.1c

Fig.3a

Fig.3b

Fig.3c

Fig.3d

5th ROYAL INNISKILLING DRAGOON GUARDS

No.1 Dress

Forage Cap – All Ranks wore a dark green cap, with a primrose band and welt around the crown. The cap badge was on a green outline backing.

Jacket – Blue, with shoulder chains. All Ranks had collar badges, with different patterns being worn by Other Ranks and Officers. Chevrons and WOs badges were originally gold on blue. However, at a later date, these were replaced by gold on scarlet version, the chevrons also being decorated with shamrock lace. NCOs also had a metal regimental arm badge, on ba black backing. Officers used standard gilt and enamel rank badges.

Trousers – All Ranks wore green trousers, with a single 1¾ in. wide primrose yellow stripe.

No.2 Dress

Other Ranks wore the issue pattern, with collar badges, shoulder titles and a white lanyard around the left arm. The trousers were plain green.

Officers wore the whipcord, cavalry pattern, Service Dress, with collar badges and wire embroidered rank badges. A Sam Browne belt, with a whistle and plain green trousers completed this order.

No.5 Dress – Battledress

Other Ranks had collar badges, shoulder titles and a white lanyard in this order of dress. Officers wore collar badges and embroidered rank badges, on a yellow backing.

No.10 Dress – Temperate Mess Dress

Other Ranks – 1939 Pattern jacket, in scarlet, with Royal Blue roll collar and cuffs. Shoulder straps were edged with gold $^3/_{32}$ inch gimp and fastened with a small button. The front was fastened with one small button on the right front, which was secured to a small button inside the right front. Collar badges and rank badges were similar to those worn on No.1 Dress, while NCOs wore their metal regimental arm badge. No.1 Dress trousers were used, with a dark green, art silk, cummerbund.

Officers – 1902 Pattern jacket, similar in colour to that worn by the Other Ranks, but much more ornate and with a stand collar. The shoulder straps were scarlet cloth edges, with gold russia braid and silver embroidered badges of rank. Green overalls, with a primrose stripe, 2¼ inches wide, were used by Officers with this order of dress.

No.14 Dress Shirt Sleeve Order

Fig.1a Illustrates a trooper in Shirt Sleeve Order, with **Fig.1b** showing the details of the cap badge and backing. **Fig.1c** Shows details of the locket buckle on this stable belt.

Fig.2a Shows the Other Ranks' beret, with metal badge. **Fig.2b** Shows the Other Ranks' embroidered beret badge. **Fig.2c** Illustrates the shoulder title on Other Ranks' No.2 Dress. **Fig.2c** Shows the collar badge. **Fig.2d** Detail of Officer's rank slide, for wear on Shirt Sleeve Order. Only in this form of dress do officers wear an embroidered version of the shoulder title. **Fig.2e** Later pattern stable belt, which differs from the previous pattern only in the substitution of two single pronged roller,buckles and straps, in place of the locket buckle.

Other Items of Dress

Side hat – Buff body, piped gold, with a buff blue *tip* and green peak. The flaps are green, piped gold and two buttons are worn on the front.

5th ROYAL INNISKILLING DRAGOON GUARDS

Fig.1a

Fig.1b

Fig.1c

Fig.2a

Fig.2d

Fig.2b

Fig.2c

Fig.2e

Fig.2f

3rd KING'S OWN HUSSARS

No.1 Dress
Forage Cap – All Ranks wore a scarlet cap, with scarlet band and welts and a metal cap badge.
Jacket – Blue, with shoulder chains and metal collar badges for All Ranks. Other Ranks had the standard pattern jacket, with scarlet gorget patches. Officers used the cavalry pattern jacket, with plain patch breast pockets and a scarlet collar. Chevrons and WOs badges were gold on scarlet, NCOs wore a metal regimental arm badge, on a garter blue backing. Officers used small rank badges, also on garter blue backings.
Trousers – All Ranks wore blue trousers, with double yellow stripes, ¾ inch wide and $^1/_8$ inch apart.

Fig.1a cap badge, **Fig.1b** scarlet forage cap, **Fig.1c** collar badge, **Fig.1d** metal shoulder title and **Fig.1e** NCOs arm badge.

No.10 Dress – Temperate Mess Dress
For officers, a blue cloth jacket, with scarlet roll collar and pointed blue cuffs. Collar badges were worn on the lapels and metal badges of rank on the shoulder straps. The mess vest, or waistcoat, was blue and open at the front. It did not have a collar and was fastened with four small buttons.

4th QUEEN'S OWN HUSSARS

No.1 Dress
Forage Cap – All Ranks wore a red cap, with red band and welts. Other Ranks had a metal cap badge, but officers used an embroidered cap badge.
Jacket – Blue with shoulder chains, All Ranks wore metal collar badges. For Other Ranks, a standard pattern jacket, while officers used the cavalry pattern jacket, with plain patch breast pockets. Chevrons and WOs badges were gold on scarlet, while NCOs wore an embroidered regimental arm badge.
Trousers – All Ranks wore blue trousers, with double yellow stripes, ¾ inch wide and $^1/_8$ inch apart.

Fig.1a cap badge, **Fig.1b** blue beret, **Fig.1c** collar badge, **Fig.1d** metal shoulder title and **Fig.1e** NCOs arm badge.

No.10 Dress – Temperate Mess Dress
Officers wore a blue cloth jacket, with a yellow roll collar and pointed yellow cuffs. Collar badges were worn on the lapels and metal badges of rank on the shoulder straps. The mess vest, or waistcoat, was scarlet and opened at the front. It did not have a collar and was fastened with four small buttons.

3rd KING'S OWN HUSSARS

Fig.1a

Fig.1b

Fig.1c

Fig.1d

Fig.1e

4th-QUEEN'S OWN HUSSARS

Fig.1a

Fig.1b

Fig.1c

Fig.1d

Fig.1e

7th QUEEN'S OWN HUSSARS

No.1 Dress

Forage Cap – All Ranks wore a red cap with a red band and welt around the crown. Other Ranks used a metal cap badge, while Officers had an embroidered cap badge.
Jacket – Blue, with shoulder chains and All Ranks wearing metal collar badges. Chevrons and WOs badges were gold on scarlet. NCOs also wore an embroidered regimental arm badge. Officers wore standard rank badges.
Trousers – All Ranks had blue trousers, with double yellow stripes ¾ inch wide and $^{1}/_{8}$ inch apart.

Fig.1a – shows the Other Ranks' forage cap and badge. **Fig.1b** illustrates the OR's bi-metal collar badge, while **Fig.1c** is the OR's shoulder title. **Fig.2a** is the *Maid of Warsaw* arm badge, worn by all ranks in recognition of the 7th Hussars' support of the Second Polish Corps, during the 2WW Italian campaign. **Fig.2b** illustrates the NCOs regimental arm badge. **Fig.2c** is the cloth shoulder title worn by Officers on Service Dress, Battledress and Greatcoats.

Other Items of Dress

Stable belt – (from top to bottom) Oxford blue, yellow, Oxford blue, yellow, Oxford blue, yellow, Oxford blue. Over the years, various fasteners were used with this belt. These included a chromed version of the web belt fastener, or single buckled versions, with leather straps.

8th KING'S ROYAL IRISH HUSSARS

No.1 Dress

Forage Cap – All Ranks wore a red cap with a red band and welt around the crown. Other Ranks used a metal cap badge, while Officers had different pattern of regimental badge.
Jacket – Blue, with shoulder chains, with All Ranks wearing metal collar badges. WOs badges were gold on scarlet and NCOs chevrons were gold shamrock lace, on scarlet. NCOs also wore a metal regimental arm badge. Officers used standard rank badges, in non-enamelled gilt.
Trousers – All Ranks had blue trousers, with double yellow stripes ¾ inch wide and $^{1}/_{8}$ inch apart.

No.5 Dress – Battledress

Fig.1a Shows a 2/Lt, serving in the 4th Infantry Division, wearing 1949 Pattern BD, c.1957. Officers had the exposed plastic buttons on their battledress replaced with leather, "football type" buttons. They also wore cloth shoulder titles, with rank badges embroidered on yellow. **Fig.1b** illustrates the special 'tent' hat worn by Officers, with this and other orders of dress. Other Ranks had brass shoulder titles and a unique green plaited lanyard on their right shoulder. **Fig.2a** is the ORs cap badge, **Fig.2b** ORs collar badges and **Fig.2c** is their gilding metal shoulder title.

Other Items of Dress

Stable belt – This was emerald green, fastened with either one, or two, single pronged buckles and brown leather straps.

7th QUEEN'S OWN HUSSARS

Fig.1b

Fig.1a

Fig.1c

Fig.2a

Fig.2b

Fig.2c

8th KING'S ROYAL IRISH HUSSARS

Fig.1b

Fig.1c

Fig.1d

Fig.1a

10th ROYAL HUSSARS

No.1 Dress
Forage Cap – All Ranks wore a red cap, with a red band and welt around the crown, with a metal cap badge.
Jacket – Blue, with shoulder chains, All Ranks had metal collar badges and shoulder titles. Chevrons and Wos' badges were gold on scarlet, NCOs also used an embroidered regimental arm badge. Officers' rank badges were standard gilt without enamel.
Trousers – All Ranks, blue trousers, with double yellow stripes, ¾ inch wide and $^{1}/_{8}$ inch apart.

No.2 Dress – Service Dress
Fig.1a Illustrates a captain wearing Service Dress, with a khaki forage cap. This is a cavalry pattern jacket, having plain patch breast pockets, inset side pockets and rectangular buttoned flaps. The front was fitted with ball buttons and collar badges were not worn. The cuffs are pointed, open at the sides and fastened with two buttons. He is wearing the ribbons of the Defence Medal, War Medal 1939-45 and General Service Medal. **Fig.1b** Shows the shoulder strap, which is fitted with plain rank stars and shoulder titles, both gilt. **Fig.1c** Depicts the Other Ranks' cap badge, which was worn on a red backing on the blue beret. **Fig.1d** Shows the Other Ranks' collar badge, worn on No.1 Dress.

Other Items of Dress
Stable belt – (top to bottom) unequal stripes of maroon, white and black and fastened with a single brown leather strap and pronged buckle.

11th HUSSARS

Fig.1a – Illustrates a 2/Lt in No.1 Dress. Officers' cap badges were in gilt, while Other Ranks had a gilding metal, or later an anodised, cap badge. The buttons have St Edward's (Queen's) crown and the ribbon is for the General Service Medal. **Fig.1b** Shows the standard pattern of shoulder chains, with the small pattern of gilt rank stars **Fig.1c** Is a close-up of the gold embroidered collar badge, worn by Sergeants and above. **Fig.1d** Illustrate the overalls for officers in No.1 Dress, Other Ranks wearing plain crimson trousers. The origins of the crimson trousers date back to 1840, when the regiment escorted Prince Albert from Dover, for his marriage to Queen Victoria. Crimson was the colour of Prince Albert's livery.

No.1 Dress
Forage Cap – All ranks wore a crimson cap, with a crimson band and welts.
Jacket – Blue, with shoulder chains. Junior ranks had metal collar badges, with gold embroidered collar badges for Sergeants and above. Chevrons and Wos' badges are of gold on crimson. NCOs also used an embroidered regimental arm badge. Officers had small rank badges, gilt without enamel.
Trousers – Other Ranks, crimson trousers without stripes and crimson trousers with double yellow stripes ¾-in wide and ½-in apart for Officers.

10th ROYAL HUSSARS

Fig.1a

Fig.1b

Fig.1c

Fig.1d

11th HUSSARS

Fig.1a

Fig.1b

Fig.1c

Fig.1d

Fig.2a Illustrates the same 2/Lt, at Fig. 1a, but in Service Dress. On this occasion, he has a khaki forage cap, with bronze cap badge. Originally, a universal pattern Service Dress jacket, in khaki whipcord, was worn post-war. This gave way to a cavalry pattern jacket, also made in khaki whipcord, which had plain patch breast pockets and inset side pockets. **Fig.2b** Shows the bronze collar badge, similar to the cap badge, but smaller. **Fig.2c** Details the rank badge, in bronze, to match the cap and collar badges. **Fig.2d** The jacket is worn with plain crimson trousers, without turn ups. Other Ranks wore the standard issue Pattern No.2 Dress, which was introduced in the early 1960s. The jacket had flat, gold anodised buttons, with a white lanyard on the left shoulder.

No.5 Dress – Battledress
Fig.3a Is again the same 2/Lt, in issue 1949 Pattern battledress, with khaki forage cap and bronze badge. As with Service Dress, his collar and rank badges are of bronze. To enhance this uniform, brown leather golf ball type buttons have replaced all the exposed plastic buttons on the blouse, also on the hip and map pockets of his battledress trousers. **Fig.3b** Are the formation signs of the Royal Armoured Corps Training Brigade. This consists of the Torch of Learning, in a mailed fist, on a blue background. Battledress worn by Other Ranks was not fitted with leather buttons. It had gilding metal, or anodised, collar badges. **Fig.4a** Shows the gilding metal shoulder strap title, worn by ORs, while Fig.**4b** Shows the NCOs' arm badge, which was not only much larger than the cap badge, but was also made from silver, or white metal. ORs also wore a white lanyard on their left shoulder. Other Ranks and Officers, when on exercise, wore a special regimental pattern of beret. This was brown, with a one inch crimson band. No badge is worn on this very distinctive headdress. **Fig.4c** Is the embroidered No.1 Dress NCOs arm badge.

No.10 Dress – Temperate Mess Dress
Other Ranks – dark blue 1939 Pattern jacket, with crimson cloth roll collar and cuffs. It had twisted gold cord shoulder cords, with small buttons. The jacket fastened with two linked large buttons and it also had three large buttons down each side of the front. Collar badges, NCOs' arm badges and No.1 Dress rank and chevron badges were worn. A crimson cloth cummerbund, 4½-inches wide, with No.1 Dress trousers, completed this order of dress.
Officer - Jacket, blue, with a crimson collar, decorated with gold lace around the collar and cuffs, down the front and around the bottom of the jacket. The shoulder straps were made from plain gold braid, on a blue backing. Silver wire embroidered rank badges were worn on the shoulder straps. The mess vest was crimson, decorated with gold braid down the front, also along the bottom, but only for three inches either side. The pockets were decorated with gold braid, with crows feet at either end. Officers used No.1 Dress overalls, with double yellow stripes.

No.11 Dress – Tropical Mess Dress
Other Ranks – 1939 Pattern, white *sharkskin*, with roll collar, pointed cuffs and shoulder straps of the same colour. The badges and buttons were similar to those worn on No.10 Dress.

Other Items of Dress
Stable belt – crimson web, with a narrower, central stripe of medium yellow. The belt was fastened with a brown leather strap and a single pronged, leather covered buckle.
Side hat – Crimson body, piped gold, with a crimson peak and tip and crimson flaps also piped gold. It was fitted with two small regimental buttons and a wire embroidered badge.

Fig.2c

Fig.2a

Fig.2c

Fig.2d

Fig.4a

Fig.4b

Fig.c

Fig.3a

Fig.3b

13th/18th HUSSARS

No.1 Dress

Forage Cap – All ranks wore a white cap, with a blue band and welt around the crown.
Jacket – Blue, with shoulder chains, the Officers with 13/18RH brass titles on their shoulder chains. All Ranks had white gorget patches, with white metal collar badges. Chevrons and Wos' badges were of gold, on white and NCOs had an embroidered regimental arm badge. Officers used standard rank badges.
Trousers – For All Ranks were blue, with double white stripes, ¾-in wide and $^1/_8$-inch apart. Regimentally, the white stripes are coloured *buff.*

No.5 Dress – Battledress

Fig.1a Sergeant in 1949 Pattern BD c.1956. The dark blue beret has a gilding metal cap badge, with a St Edward's (Queen's) Crown. This was one of the smallest cap badges worn in the British Army. He also has matching collar badges and a white lanyard around his right arm. The medal ribbon is that of the General Service Medal, probably issued with the Malaya clasp, as the regiment were engaged in this campaign in the late 1940s and early 1950s. **Fig.1b** Shows the gilding metal (brass) 13/18H shoulder titles, worn on both shoulder straps. On his left arm is the regimental white and dark blue flash, which was originally adopted by the 13th Hussars, during the Boer War 1899-1902, as a pagri (puggaree) flash on their Foreign Service helmets. **Fig.1c** Is the cap badge, which is identical to the collar badges, but with a slider fitting for wear in the hat, or beret, while the collar badges have loop fittings. **Fig.1d** Shows the NCOs' arm badge, worn on the chevrons of the right arm. It consists of an entwined QMO monogram - Queen Mary's Own. This had been originally worn by the 18th Hussars, being introduced in 1911.

Fig.2a NCOs arm badge, as worn on Mess Dress. **Fig.2b** Is the Other Ranks' forage cap, worn with both No.1 and No.2 Dress. **Fig.2c** Is the cap badge worn on the DPM helmet cover of the Mk.6 combat helmet. **Fig.2d** Shows the anodised shoulder title worn on No.2 Dress by Other Ranks. This is not as tall as the gilding metal version, worn on battledress. **Fig.2e** Is the regimental pattern stable belt. **Fig.2f** Is an olive green rank slide, in this case for the Lt-Colonel.

No.10 Dress – Temperate Mess Dress

Other Ranks – 1902 Pattern jacket, of dark blue cloth, with matching stand collar and plain cuffs. White gorget patches on the collar, fitted with collar badges. The jacket had no shoulder cords, or shoulder straps. The inside of the front and front edges are lined with Cossack Green cloth. The front is open, with no buttons. Rank badges and chevrons were of the No.1 Dress type, but smaller. This was complemented by a dark blue silk cummerbund, fastened by three pairs of hooks and eyes, together with No.1 Dress trousers.
Officers – 1902 Pattern jacket, similar to the Other Ranks' pattern, but with a white collar, and triangular white cuffs, both trimmed with gold lace. It also had gold plaited shoulder cords, with silver embroidered rank badges.

Other Items of Dress

Side hat - This had a white body, with gold piping, a dark blue peak and white tip. The dark blue flaps were also piped in gold. It was fitted with two regimental buttons and a metal cap badge. The Other Ranks' side cap was similar, except that it did not have the gold piping of the officers' version.

13th/18th HUSSARS

Fig.1c

Fig.1d

Fig.1a

Fig.1b

Fig.2a

Fig.2b

Fig.2c

Fig.2d

Fig.2e

Fig.2f

14th/20th KING'S HUSSARS

No.1 Dress

Forage Cap – All ranks wore a red cap, with a red band and welt around the crown.

Jacket – Blue, with shoulder chains, all ranks had collar badges. Chevrons and Wos' badges were originally gold on yellow, later changed to gold on scarlet. A metal regimental arm badge was authorised for NCOs and All Ranks had the regimental crossed kukri arm badge. Officers used standard badges of rank.

Trousers – for All Ranks were blue, with double yellow stripes, ¾-in wide and ⅛-inch apart.

No.10 Dress – Temperate Mess Dress

Other Ranks – 1939 Pattern jacket, in dark blue cloth, with a blue silk faced roll collar, fitted with collar badges. It had dark blue, pointed cuffs, with no shoulder straps. The embroidered crossed kukris were worn 1-inch from the top of each sleeve. The jacket had no buttons on it The rank badges were originally similar to those worn on No.1 Dress, but smaller. These were later changed to a gold cord, rope style, on a scarlet backing. The mess vest was white cotton, fastened with four engraved, gilt flat buttons.

Fig.1a Corporal in Mess Dress. **Fig.1b** insignia worn on his right arm. **Fig.1c** Collar badge. **Fig.1d** Miniature Campaign Service Medal, with Northern Ireland bar. **Fig.1e** Pointed cuff and trouser stripes.

Officers – 1902 Pattern jacket in dark blue, with a stand collar, which had 3/16-inch Russia gimp around top and front of collar. The collar fastened with gold Russia gimp. The jacket had double gold shoulder cords, with plain buttons. The rear of the jacket was embellished with gold Russia gimp. The cuffs were decorated with two crow's feet and two double barrels, also in gold Russia gimp. The 1902 Pattern vest was scarlet, fastened with a zip and the stand collar fastens with hooks and eyes. The front was decorated with six sets of gold gimp frogging and six buttons.

Fig.2a Gilding metal cap badge, **Fig.2b** Officers' wire embroidered beret badge, **Fig.2c** Black and gold cap badge, introduced in 1969. On the blue beret it was worn on an oval primrose backing, to make it stand out. **Fig.2d** In 1979 an embroidered Other Ranks' beret badge was introduced.

Fig.3a NCO's regimental arm badge. This pattern was worn only by Lance Corporals. **Fig.3b** NCOs' regimental arm badge, worn by all other NCOs and WOs.

Other Items of Dress

Side hat – Officers, scarlet body, piped gold and with a scarlet peak and tip. The scarlet flaps were also piped gold. It had two engraved gilt buttons and an embroidered badge. Warrant Officers and Sergeants had a similar version, but with gold gimp instead of piping. It was fitted with issue regimental buttons and a metal badge. Corporals and below wore a similar version to the Warrant Officers' pattern, but without the gimp.

Stable belt – three equal one inch stripes of blue, yellow and blue webbing. The belt was fastened with two nickel plated, single prong, roller type buckles, which fastened to tan leather straps.

14th/20th KING'S HUSSARS

Fig.1a

Fig.1c

Fig.1d

Fig.1b

Fig.1e

Fig.2a

Fig.2b

Fig.2c

Fig.3a

Fig.2d

Fig.3b

15th/19th KING'S ROYAL HUSSARS

No.1 Dress

Forage Cap – All ranks wore a scarlet cap, with a scarlet band and welt around the crown.
Jacket – Blue, with rectangular shoulder chains, the latter being converted regimentally from the issue "bastion" pattern. These are claimed to be a reminder of the time when chain mail burnishers were worn on the shoulders. The collar on the officers' jacket was decorated with gold Austrian lace. Chevrons and WOs' badges were gold on scarlet. NCOs had an embroidered regimental arm badge, in silver on scarlet. All Officers used standard badges of rank, without enamel.
Trousers – All Ranks, blue trousers, with double yellow stripes, ¾-in wide and $^1/_8$-inch apart.

Fig.1a 2/Lt's No.1 Dress jacket. This is the standard pattern for the most part. It has box pleated breast pockets and plain patch side pockets, all of which had three-pointed flaps, which fastened with a small regimental button. The cuffs are pointed and the vents are closed with two buttons. The front and top of the collar are edged with gold lace, while the base of the collar is decorated with gold gimp cord. Collar badges are not worn by Officers on this order of dress. **Fig.1b** Right rectangular shoulder strap(chain?) showing rank star and Officers' pattern of shoulder title. **Fig.2** Field Officers' forage cap, with gold *passing* on the front of the peak.

Fig.2a Gold lace pouch belt, edged with scarlet cloth and worn by all Officers in No.1 Dress. The buckle tip and slides are gilt. **Fig.2b** Victorian pattern gilt tip, which were still being worn by some officers into the 1950s. **Fig.2c** Victorian pattern pouch, worn with pouch belt. This is scarlet in colour and decorated mainly with gold embroidery. A similar pattern with a Tudor (King's) crown was also worn. Some officers were unable to obtain one of these ornate pouches and wore instead a plain black pouch, without a badge.

No.10 Dress – Temperate Mess Dress

Fig.3a Squadron Quarter-Master Sergeant in 1939 Pattern Mess Dress. On his left lapel, above the collar badge, is the miniature version of the Compaign Service Medal, probably issued for service in Northern Ireland. **Fig.3b** Lower right arm rank badge and NCOs' arm badge. The scarlet pointed cuffs fitted with two buttons at the rear seam. Also note the double yellow striped trousers. **Fig.3c** Cord shoulder strap, with gold anodised regimental button. **Fig.3d** Linked regimental buttons, used to fasten the front of the jacket. **Fig.1e** Small gilt collar badge, for Mess Dress of senior NCOs and Warrant Officers. A scarlet silk cummerbund, with three pleats, completed this order of dress.

Fig.4a Major, 1902 pattern jacket, dark blue, with a dark blue stand collar. The upper edges of the collar and the front and bottom edges of the jacket were trimmed with gold lace.The lower edge of the collar was trimmed with gold piping and it fastened with two hooks and eyes. The upper edges of the scarlet pointed cuffs were trimmed with gold piping. Collar badges were not worn. **Fig.4b** Blue cloth shoulder strap, with regimental button and small, gilt rank badge. **Fig.4c** Mess vest. This consists of a scarlet, false front, fastening at the neck and around the waist with elastic. The front is decorated with a double row of gold piping, while the the top and bottom edges are decorated with a single row. A cummerbund is not worn by officers in this order of dress.

15th/19th KING'S ROYAL HUSSARS

Fig.2

Fig.1a

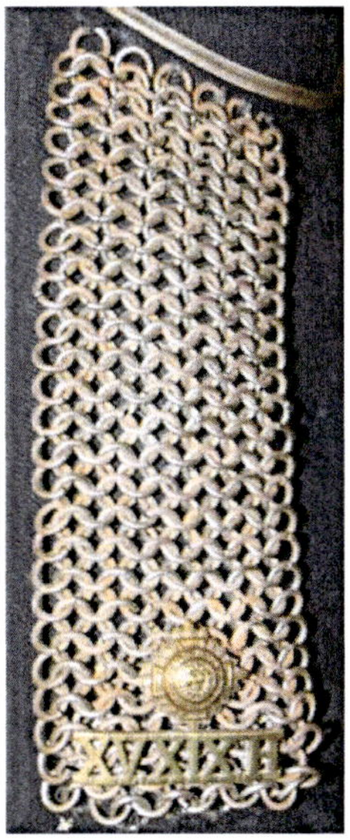

Fig.1b

Fig.2c

Fig.2a

Fig.2b

No.11 Dress – Tropical Mess Dress
Other Ranks – 1939 Pattern, in white drill, with a roll collar and pointed cuffs. The gold cord shoulder straps were fastened with two regimental buttons. Like the temperate version, it had two buttons on each cuff and fastened at the front with two linked regimental buttons.

No.13 Dress – Temperate barrack dress
Fig.5a Officers' regimental pattern of pullover, used in Temperate Barrack Dress. This consists of a khaki woollen, plain knit pullover, with a crew neck. It has oval sleeve patches and imitation shoulder straps, both made from khaki barathea material. **Fig.5b** Shoulder strap showing captain's rank stars, embroidered on yellow, with embroidered shoulder title. **Fig.5c** Embroidered Officer's pattern shoulder title, also worn on removable rank slides.

Fig.6 Other Ranks' issue dark blue beret, with a red felt backing to the badge. **Fig.7** Officers' side hat, with scarlet body, piped gold and with a scarlet peak and tip. The scarlet flaps were also piped gold. It had two buttons at the front and the officers wore an embroidered badge. The Other Ranks' side hat had a scarlet body, flaps, tip and peak. It was fitted with two buttons and a metal badge. Warrant Officers had yellow piping on the body, flaps and peak of their hat. Staff Sergeants and Sergeants had yellow piping on just the body and flaps. Corporals and below had yellow piping on the body only.

Fig.8a Other Ranks' bi-metal cap badge, with Tudor (King's) crown. **Fig.8b** Other Ranks' gold and silver anodised cap badge, with St Edward's (Queen's) crown. **Fig.8c** Officers' embroidered badge, worn on both the beret and side hat. **Fig.9a** Other Ranks' bi-metal Tudor crown collar badge. **Fig.9b** Other Ranks', anodised St Edward's crown collar badge. **Fig.10a** Other Rsanks'gilding metal shoulder title for battledress. **Fig.10b** Other Ranks' gold anodised No.2 Dress shoulder title.

Fig.11a NCOs' regimental arm badge, the wire embroidered version was worn on No.1 Dress and Mess Dress. **Fig.11b** NCOs' regimental arm badge, this embroidered version was worn on No.2 Dress.

Other Items of Dress
Fig.12 Dress belt. This was brown plastic, 1¾ inches wide, with brass plate and white metal embellishments and was worn by Other Ranks with No.2 Dress.

Fig.13 Stable belt. Dark blue 1-inch, yellow ½-inch, scarlet ½-inch and dark blue 1-inch, fastened with tan leather straps.

Fig.3d

Fig.3e

Fig.3a

Fig.3b

Fig.3c

Fig.4a

Fig.4c

Fig.4b

Fig.5a

Fig.5b

Fig.5c

Fig.6

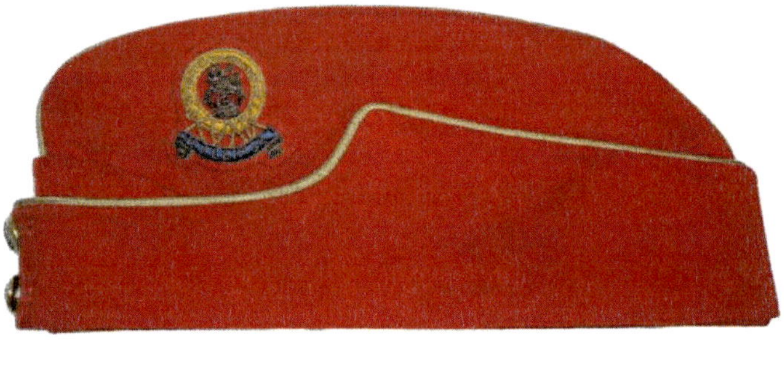

Fig.7

Fig.8a

Fig.8b

Fig.8c

Fig.9a

Fig.8d

Fig.9b

Fig.11a

Fig.10b

Fig.10a

Fig.11b

Fig.12

Fig.13

1st KING'S DRAGOON GUARDS

No.1 Dress

Forage Cap – All ranks wore a blue cap, with a blue band and welt around the crown.
Jacket – Blue, with shoulder chains, all ranks had collar badges. Chevrons and WOs badges were gold on blue. NCOs used a metal regimental arm badge on a red backing. Officers had standard patterns of rank badges.
Trousers – All Ranks wore blue trousers with single yellow stripe, 1¾-in wide.

No.5 Dress – Battledress

In 1956, the 1st King's Dragoon Guards were stationed in Malaya. **Fig.1a** Shows a Lieutenant wearing a tailor-made battledress. Based on the original 1937 pattern, it is in much better material and is lined. He has silver collar badges and the ribbon for the General Service Medal, possibly for his service in Malaya. **Fig.1b** Illustrates the unusual form of rank insignia used by KDG officers. Rank stars and crowns have a yellow backing, which varied in length depending on the number of rank badges worn. **Fig.1c** 17th Gurkha Division formation sign. While serving in Malaya the KDG were assigned to the 17th Gurkha Division, with Squadrons attached to the 26 Gurkha Brigade, 99 Gurkha Brigade and Selangor Troops. Other Ranks wore a blue beret, gilding metal shoulder titles and a white lanyard. Cpls and above wore a metal regimental NCOs arm badge, on a red pear shaped backing, on their right arm.

Fig.2a Other Ranks cap badge **Fig.2b** Forage cap, this pattern was also worn by the Royal Signals and the Military Provost Staff Corps. **Fig.2c** Other Ranks collar badge, **Fig.2d** Gilding metal shoulder title, as used on Battledress. **Fig.2e** NCOs regimental arm badge, on its red pear shaped backing, for corporal, sergeants and Warrant Officers.

No.10 Dress – Temperate Mess Dress

Officers – 1939 pattern jacket, scarlet with a blue roll collar. The blue pointed cuffs were 6 inches deep at the point and 2¾ inches deep at the back. The shoulder straps were scarlet, tapering from 1½ inches at the seam, to 1 inch at the point and fastening with a regimental button, with metal badges of rank. There were no buttons on the front of the jacket, not did it have any gold braid, or piping. Collar badges were worn on the lapels. The vest, or waistcoat, was also scarlet, open at the front and without a collar. It was fastened with four regimental buttons.

1st KING'S DRAGOON GUARDS

Fig.1c

Fig.1a

Fig.1b

Fig.2a

Fig.2b

Fig.2e

Fig.2c

Fig.2d

KING'S ROYAL HUSSARS

No.1 Dress
Forage Cap – All ranks wear a crimson cap, with a crimson band and welt around the crown. All officers, irrespective of rank, had ¾-inch gold *passing* on the peak of the cap.
Jacket – Blue, with shoulder chains, all ranks wearing the large 10th Hussars pattern collar badges. Chevrons and WOs badges are gold on crimson. NCOs have a metal regimental arm badge. All Ranks also wear gold embroidered crossed kukri arm badges. Officers used standard badges of rank badges.
Trousers – Other Ranks wear crimson trousers, without stripes and Officers crimson trousers, with ¾-in wide double yellow stripes, ½-in apart.

Fig.1a LCpl wearing No.1 Dress. Note the ribbons for the Campaign Service Medal (Northern Ireland) and the NATO medal for Former Yugoslavia. **Fig.1b** insignia on his right arm, including the metal NCO's arm badge, previously used by the 14th/20th King's Hussars. **Fig.1c** Embroidered regimental arm badge, worn on both arms. **Fig.1d** Shows the plain crimson trousers for with this order of dress.

Fig.2a Trooper in 1980 Pattern No.2 Dress, with small pattern collar badges. **Fig.2b** Insignia on his left arm, including white lanyard, metal shoulder title and crossed kukris. **Fig.2c** Silver anodised crossed kukris, worn on both arms. **Fig.2d** Shows the plain crimson trousers for this order of dress.

Fig.3a Staff Sergeant wearing No.3 Dress. **Fig.3b** Ribbons for the Gulf Medal, with rosette denoting clasp for August 1990 – January 1991, Campaign Service Medal (Northern Ireland) NATO Medal for Former Yugoslavia, NATO Medal for Kosovo and the Army Long Service and Good Conduct Medal. **Fig.3c** All Ranks flat gilt button. **Fig.3d** Insignia on the right arm.

No.5 Dress – Desert combat dress
Fig.4a Trooper in the desert version of Soldier '95, note the slotted buttons. **Fig.4b** KRH tactical recognition flash, worn on the right arm. **Fig.4c** Union flag and subdued version of the 12th Mechanized Brigade, worn on his left arm. **Fig.4d** Coloured version 12th Mechanized Brigade formation sign, for the DPM combat jacket.

No.13 Dress – Temperate barrack dress
Fig.5a Lance Corporal wearing a modified issue jersey. The green shoulder straps have been removed and replaced with detachable crimson shoulder straps. These are also fitted with regimental shoulder titles and buttons. Note the brown beret with crimson "tombstone" badge backing. **Fig.5b** Insignia on the right arm, **Fig.5c** Shoulder strap. **Fig.5d** Other Ranks embroidered beret badge.

Fig.6a Other Ranks' cap badge, **Fig.6b** Shoulder title, **Fig.6c** Small collar badge, worn on No.2 Dress, **Fig.6d** Large collar badge worn on No.1 and No.3 Dress. **Fig.7** Corporals' rank slide, **Fig.8** Stable belt.

Other Items of Dress
Regimental pullover – WOs and Senior NCOs wear a brown, crimson, green and black knitted pullover. It has a round neck, with crimson shoulder and elbow pads. The crimson epaulettes have KRH embroidered in primrose.

KING'S ROYAL HUSSARS

Fig.1a

Fig.1c

Fig.1b

Fig.1d

Fig.2a

Fig.2c

Fig.2b

Fig.2d

Fig.3a

Fig.3b

Fig.3c

Fig.3d

Fig.4a

Fig.4b

Fig.4c

Fig.4d

Fig.5d

Fig.5a

Fig.5b

Fig.5c

Fig.6a

Fig.6c

Fig.6b

Fig.7

Fig.6d

Fig.8

9th QUEEN'S ROYAL LANCERS

No.1 Dress

Forage Cap – All Ranks wore a blue cap, with a scarlet band and welt around the crown. In imitation of czapka helmets, it also had scarlet quarter welts. Other Ranks used a metal cap badge, while Officers had an embroidered cap badge.

Jacket – Blue, with shoulder chains, the latter fitted with metal shoulder titles. The collar of the Other Ranks' jacket was fitted with scarlet gorget patches, which had rounded ends. However, from July 1958 to August 1960, gorget patches were not worn. ORs had collar badges, whilst Officers wore jackets with a scarlet collar, without collar badges. Chevrons and WOs badges were gold on scarlet. NCOs also had a metal regimental arm badge. Officers rank badges were standard gilt, without enamel.

Trousers – All Ranks had blue trousers, with double yellow stripes ¾ inch wide and $^1/_8$ inch apart.

Fig.1a Other Ranks' cap badge and **Fig.1b** Other Ranks collar badge. **Fig.1c** Officers' forage cap badge. **Fig.1d** Ordnance issue shoulder title, not worn. **Fig.1e** Regimental shoulder title, which all were obliged to purchase, used on battledress and No.1 Dress. **Fig.1f** NCOs regimental arm badge, for corporals to the RSM, on battledress and No.1 Dress. **Fig.1g** regimental arm badge, worn by all on both arms of the battledress. Regimentally called scarlet and old gold, these are worn in pairs, with the yellow part of the upper strip facing the front. **Fig.1h** Stable belt, other than brown leather straps it did not have any other adjustment buckles.

12th ROYAL LANCERS (Princess of Wales's)

No.1 Dress

Forage Cap – All Ranks wore a scarlet cap, with a scarlet band. It also had a blue welt around the crown and blue quarter welts, in imitation of the czapka. All Ranks used a metal cap badge.

Jacket – Other Ranks wore a blue jacket, with shoulder chains and Officers a blue, cavalry type jacket, with shoulder chains and plain breast pockets. The seams on the back of this jacket, together with those on the back of the sleeves, were also piped in red. This echoed the piping on the old Lancer jackets. All ranks used collar badges, with metal shoulder titles on the shoulder chains. Chevrons and WOs' badges were gold on scarlet. NCOs also had an embroidered regimental arm badge. An embroidered armoured car badge was introduced in about 1955, for Other Ranks. Officers' shoulder chains had embroidered rank badges.

Trousers – All Ranks, blue trousers, with double yellow stripes ¾ inch wide and $^1/_8$ inch apart.

Fig.1a Cap badge, **Fig.1b** Forage cap. The collar badge is identical in design, but slightly smaller than the cap badge. **Fig.2a** Ordnance issue shoulder title, not worn. **Fig.2b** Regimental shoulder title, which soldiers were obliged to purchase, used on battledress and No.1 Dress. **Fig.3a** NCO's regimental pattern arm badge for L/Cpls and above on battledress. **Fig.3b** NCO's battledress arm badge, between 1958 – 60. A wire embroidered version of this badge was worn on No.1 and No.3 Dress. **Fig.4** "Crewman" badge, worn by all Other Ranks on battledress, with an embroidered version for No.1 and No.3 Dress.

9th QUEEN'S ROYAL LANCERS

Fig.1a

Fig.1b

Fig.1c

Fig.1d

Fig.1e

Fig.1f

Fig.1g

Fig.1h

12th ROYAL LANCERS (Princess of Wales's)

Fig.1a

Fig.1b

Fig.2a

Fig.2b

Fig.3a

Fig.3b

Fig.4

9th/12th ROYAL LANCERS

No.1 Dress

Forage Cap – All Ranks wore a scarlet cap, with a scarlet band. It also has a blue welt around the crown andboth edges of the band. In addition blue quarter welts, in Lancer helmet style. All Ranks had a metal cap badge.

Jacket – All Ranks, blue jacket, with shoulder chains. Other Ranks have scarlet gorget patches, with round ends, on which collar badges are worn. Officers have scarlet collars and do not wear collar badges. On the Officers' jacket the seams on the back of the jacket, together with those on the back of the sleeves, are piped in red. Chevrons and Wos' badges are gold on scarlet. Other Ranks wear an embroidered armoured car, while NCOs also have an embroidered regimental arm badge, both previously worn by the 12th Lancers. Officers use small sized, non-enamelled gilt rank badges.

Trousers – All Ranks have blue trousers, with double yellow stripes ¾ inch wide and $^1/_8$ inch apart.

Fig.1a Sergeant wearing the standard issue No.1 Dress uniform and **Fig.1b** back of jacket. **Fig.1c** ribbons for the Campaign Service Medal (Northern Ireland) United Nations medal for Former Yugoslavia, 1992-95 and the NATO medal for Former Yugoslavia. **Fig.1d** Shows rank and NCO's wire embroidered badge. **Fig.1e** Shows wire embroidered "crewman" badge, plain pointed jacket cuff and trouser stripes.

Fig.2a Major wearing No.1 Dress, collar badges are not worn and note the ribbon for the Campaign Service Medal. **Fig.2b** Shows the piping on the back of the jacket and down the rear of the sleeves. **Fig.2c** Small plain gilt rank badge and shoulder title. **Fig.2d** Plain buttoned cuffs and yellow trouser stripes.

Fig.3a L/Cpl wearing 1980 Pattern, No.2 Dress, with ribbons for the NATO medal for Former Yugoslavia, NATO medal for Kosovo and Golden Jubilee Medal, 2004. **Fig.3b** NCO's regimental arm badge on black backing. **Fig.3c** Lower right arm with metal "crewman" badge, again worn on a black backing. **Fig.3d** Left arm showing shoulder title and red and yellow lanyard.

Fig.4a Lt-Col M Hudson wearing Service Dress, officers do not wear lanyards. **Fig.4b** Shoulder strap, showing small plain gilt rank badges. Officers do not wear shoulder titles or lanyards. **Fig.4c** Officer's collar badge. Cap and collar badges are identical, except for the rear fittings. **Fig.4d** Plain cuff with two buttons.

Fig.5a Lt-Col M Hudson wearing the standard 1949 Pattern battledress. **Fig.5b** Ribbons for the Defence Medal, War Medal 1939-45 and the General Service Medal, these are also on his Service Dress uniform, see Fig.4. **Fig.5c** Regimental arm badge, previously worn by the 9th Lancers. **Fig.5d** Battledress, showing layout of the various insignia. Note the leather buttons on the breast pockets.

Fig.6a Officers beret badge **Fig.6b** Other Ranks beret and embroidered badge **Fig.6c** OR's embroidered badge for tropical combat hat. **Fig.6d** Officer's side cap badge. **Fig.6e** Captain's rank slide. **Fig.6f** Anodised OR's "crewman" badge and **Fig.6g** Gilding metal ORs "crewman" badge. **Fig.6h** Stable belt.

9th/12th ROYAL LANCERS

Fig.1c

Fig.1d

Fig.1a

Fig.1b

Fig.1e

Fig.2c

Fig.2a

Fig.2b

Fig.2d

Fig.3b

Fig.3a

Fig.3c

Fig.3d

Fig.4c

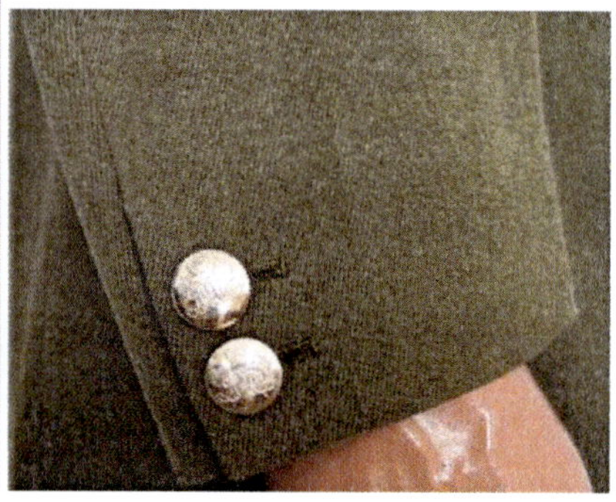

Fig.4a

Fig.4b

Fig.4d

Fig.5b

Fig.5c

Fig.5a

Fig.5d

Fig.6a

Fig.6b

Fig.6c

Fig.6d

Fig.6e

Fig.6f

Fig.6g

Fig.6h

16th/5th LANCERS

No.1 Dress

Forage Cap – All Ranks wore a scarlet cap, with a blue band. It also had a blue welt around the crown and blue quarter welts. All Ranks had a metal cap badge.

Jacket – All Ranks, blue, with shoulder chains. Collar badges for All ranks. Chevrons and WOs' badges are gold on blue. NCOs also wore a silver embroidered regimental arm badge. Officers had standard rank badges.

Trousers – All Ranks, blue trousers, with double yellow stripes ¾ inch wide and $^1/_8$ inch apart.

No.2 Dress

Fig.1a shows a Lt-Colonel, wearing Service Dress. Note the Sam Browne shoulder belt, which was worn back-to-front. This originated during a visit to the regiment by King Alfonso XIII, of Spain, who was married to Princess Ena, a grand-daughter of Queen Victoria. The Colonel, seeing the King incorrectly dressed, ordered the officers to reverse their shoulder belts, so he would not be out of place. **Fig.1b** Cap badge. **Fig.1c** Collar badge. **Fig.1d** Lt-Col's shoulder strap, with plain anodised rank badges and shoulder title.

Fig.2a Other Rank's beret badge, worn on the blue beret. **Fig.2b** Officer's beret badge. **Fig.2c** OR's embroidered badge for tropical combat hat. **Fig.3a** Collar badge, previously worn by the 16th Lancers, was worn up until the early 1950s. **Fig.3b** Collar badge, this pattern was introduced in December 1951, having previously worn by the 5th Lancers, up until 1922. This was superseded in 1955 by the pattern shown at Fig.1c. This possibly represents a compromise, so that the insignia of the 5th or 16th Lancers is not dominant over the other.

Fig.5 Lt-Col's rank slide. **Fig.6** NCO's regimental arm badge. Various wire embroidered versions of this were used on No.1 Dress, No.2 Dress and Mess Dress. **Fig.7** Stable belt.

No.10 Dress – Temperate Mess Dress

Other Ranks – 1902 Pattern jacket, of scarlet cloth, with a dark blue stand collar. It had twisted shoulder cords, fastened with two small regimental buttons. There are no buttons on the front of the jacket, or on the dark blue pointed cuffs. The seams on the back of the jacket, together with those on the back of the sleeves, are piped in blue. Collar badges were worn and the rank badges and chevrons were of the No.1 Dress type. This was worn with a scarlet art silk cummerbund, five inches wide, without pleats, and also No.1 Dress trousers.

Officers – 1902 Pattern jacket, similar to the Other Ranks' pattern. The collar is trimmed with one inch gold, scalloped edge, lace, as are the dark blue pointed cuffs. The back and rear sleeve seams are also piped in blue, like the ORs' jacket. The collar is fastened with a loop of gold russia braid. Collar badges are not worn, although the cuffs are fitted with two regimental buttons. Silver plated badges of rank are worn on the gold cord shoulder straps. The 1902 Pattern vest is dark blue with a stand collar, with a hook and eye front. It has ¾ inch French braid on part of the collar, down the front edges and along part of the bottom edges. The vest also has two *jetted* pockets.

Other Items of Dress

Side hat – This had a scarlet body, with gold piping, a dark blue peak and white tip. The dark blue flaps were also piped in gold. It was fitted with two regimental buttons and a metal cap badge.

16th/5th LANCERS

Fig.1a

Fig.1b

Fig.1c

Fig.1d

Fig.2a

Fig.2b

Fig.2c

Fig.3a

Fig.3b

Fig.4

Fig.5

Fig.6

17th/21st LANCERS

No.1 Dress

Forage Cap – All Ranks wear a blue cap, with a white band. It also has a blue welt around the crown and blue quarter welts. All Ranks had a metal cap badge.
Jacket – All Ranks, blue, with shoulder chains. All were fitted with white gorget patches, having pointed ends, on which collar badges were worn. Chevrons and WOs' badges were gold on white. Sergeants and S/Sgts wore a metal regimental NCOs' arm badge, while Warrant Officers had an embroidered version. Officers used standard rank badges.
Trousers – For All Ranks were blue, with double white stripes, ¾-in wide and $^1/_8$-inch apart. The white stripes are called buff, regimentally.

No.2 Dress

Fig.1a Shows a WO II wearing 1964 Pattern No.2 Dress. Lanyards were not worn by this regiment. **Fig.1b** Is the cap badge, which is referred to as 'The Motto' within the regiment. **Fig.1c** Collar badge. **Fig.1d** Anodised shoulder title. **Fig.1e** Lower right arm, showing rank badge and the metal NCO's arm badge.

No.8 Dress – Temperate combat dress.

Fig.2 shows a trooper in the early 1970s, dressed for Internal Security duties in Northern Ireland. All regiments, including those of the RAC, spent some time during The Troubles in Northern Ireland. He is in DPM combat dress, over which is body armour. This early pattern, made in America, had a ¾ collar and a permanently fixed cover. Later patterns had removable covers, with rubber or PVC rifle pads.

No.10 Dress – Temperate Mess Dress

Other Ranks – 1939 Pattern jacket, dark blue barathea, with a stepped collar. It had white faced collar and cuffs, both trimmed with Austrian knots, in gold Russia braid. The jacket was not fitted with shoulder straps. There were three buttons down the front of each side, with an extra button hole on each side, the jacket being closed with a pair of small linked buttons, in the manner of cuff-links. Collar badges, chevrons and rank badges were similar to those worn on No.1 Dress. The cummerbund was of dark blue art silk and worn without pleats.
Officers – 1902 Pattern dark blue jacket, with a stand collar. The collar was faced white and trimmed with 1 inch gold lace and fastened with a gold Russia loop. Field officers had double gold gimp around the bottom edge of the collar. The jacket had gold lace down both the front edges. The shoulder straps were of double gold gimp and fitted with silver embroidered badges of rank. The blue pointed cuffs were trimmed with 1 inch gold lace. The seams on the back of the jacket, together with those on the rear of the sleeves, were piped in white. A 1902 Pattern mess vest was worn under the jacket. It was French Grey in colour and had a stand collar, the collar fastening with two hooks and eyes. The front of the vest also fastened with hooks and eyes. French braid, $^3/_8$ inches wide, was fitted to the top and front edges of the collar, down the front of the vest and along the bottom edges to the seams. The vest had two pockets, which were decorated with No.4 gold Russia 'crow's feet'.

No.14 Dress – Shirt Sleeve Order

Fig.3 shows a trooper wearing Shirt Sleeve Order, in this instance consisting of blue beret, non-issue No.2 Dress shirt, stable belt and lightweight trousers. The latter were introduced in the 1970s, as an alternative to the lined combat trousers. They were very popular with the troops and were worn for a whole range of activities.

17th/21st LANCERS

Fig.1a

Fig.1b

Fig.1c

Fig.1d

Fig.1e

Fig.2

Fig.3

LIGHT DRAGOONS

No.1 Dress

Forage Cap – All Ranks wear a scarlet cap with a scarlet band and welt. All officers have ¾-inch gold braid on the peaks of their caps, irrespective of rank.
Jacket – Other Ranks, blue, with a white collar and collar badges. These are fitted with the 15th/19th Hussars unique rectangular pattern shoulder chains. The officers wear a similar jacket, but with a buff collar, the front and top edges of which are decorated with Austrian lace, no collar badges being worn. Officers' jackets were originally fitted with the rectangular shoulder chains, but are now gradually being replaced by the standard "bastion" pattern. Chevrons and WOs' badges are gold on scarlet. NCOs have a wire embroidered regimental arm badge, while Officers wear standard rank badges.
Trousers – All Ranks wear blue, with double yellow stripes, ¾-in wide and ¼-inch apart.

No.2 Dress

Fig.1a Shows a WO II Army Recruiter, wearing the 1980 Pattern No.2 Dress uniform. **Fig.1b** Ribbons for the Campaign Service Medal (Northern Ireland) and UN Cyprus Medal, which are partly, or wholly, obscured by his shoulder belt. **Fig.1c** Rear of uniform, showing his shoulder belt and pouch. **Fig.1d** Pouch belt and badge. **Fig.1e** Top of his right arm, showing anodised shoulder title, parachute for Qualified Operational Parachutist and finally wire embroidered union flags, identifying him as an Army Recruiter. **Fig.1f** Lower right arm, WO II rank badge, this is the wire embroidered version, matching his appointment badge, these being worn on both arms. Below this is the regimental NCO's arm badge, consisting of a Tudor 'King's' Crown, with a lion above, in white embroidered on scarlet. **Fig.1g** Upper left arm, showing anodised shoulder title and the regimental white and dark blue flash, previously worn by the $13^{th}/18^{th}$ Hussars. The regimental flash is made from two pieces of coloured felt.

Officers jacket – this is made from drab khaki whipcord material, in cavalry pattern style. It is single breasted, cut as a lounge coat to the waist, with a back seam. Loose fitting at the chest and shoulders, but fitted at the waist. The breast pockets are plain, without a centre pleat, and fitted with oblong flaps, with rounded corners. The waist pockets are *jetted*, also fitted with oblong flaps, which have rounded corners. The plain cuffs have a 3 inch vent, fastened with two regimental buttons. There are four large buttons down the front of the jacket, while the remainder are small. Metal collar and rank badges are worn on the jacket. The trousers are of matching material, turn-ups being worn by the Light Dragoons. The LD also wear a brown leather, regimental pattern shoulder belt, as opposed to the Sam Browne belt.

No.8 Dress – Temperate combat dress.

Fig.2a WO II wearing the so-called 1994 Pattern combat jacket, easily identified by the two vertically zippered chest pockets. It was worn with matching trousers, combat high boots, combat shirt and blue beret. **Fig.2b** 1st Armoured Division formation sign. Worn on the top right of his jacket, it is woven with a merrow edge. **Fig.2c** WO II rank badge, this pattern being introduced for wear on combat dress, prior to the introduction of CS95, which was designed for use with chest mounted rank insignia. His rank badge is worn, in its normal position, on the lower right arm. **Fig.2d** Embroidered regimental arm badge, worn on the top of his left arm.

LIGHT DRAGOONS

Fig.1a

Fig.1b

Fig.1c

Fig.1d

Fig.1e

Fig.1f

Fig.1g

No.10 Dress – Temperate Mess Dress

Other Ranks – the jacket is made from blue superfine cloth, with a buff Huntsman jacket collar. The gold shoulder cords are secured with a plain half-ball button. **Fig.3a** Front view of WO II, wearing temperate Mess Dress. **Fig.3b** Back of jacket, the back seams being decorated with single gold Russia braid. **Fig.3c** Wire embroidered collar badge. **Fig.3d** Shows the lower right arm, with his embroidered rank badge, wire embroidered NCOs regimental arm badge and the gold Russia braid cuff loop. The buff vest is fitted with four half-ball buttons. No.1 Dress trousers are worn, with double yellow stripes, ¾-in wide and ¼-inch apart.

Officers – jacket of dark blue superfine cloth, with a buff stand collar and gold cord aroud the base of the collar. The collar also has an *Austrian wave* to the top and front edges. The plain cuffs are decorated with gold cord, in an Austrian knot. The shoulder straps are are decorated with three rows of gold Russia braid, on which silver wire rank badges are worn. Five olivets are fitted to the left side of the jacket. Gold cord is also fitted to the front and bottom edges of the jacket. The buff doeskin vest has a stand collar. The body and the collar are edged in *Austrian wave*, with *double wave* at the front. All of this is piped in gold. There are five horizontal rows of double gold Russia braid, with double knots at the ends. Each row is supported with a plain half-ball button at the centre.

No.13 Dress – Temperate barrack dress

Fig.4a Regimental Sergeant Major in the approved pattern of regimental pullover, worn by WOs and Senior NCOs. This consists of a light blue, green fleck, V-neck jersey, with green elbow and shoulder patches. **Fig.4b** Shows the oval elbow patch, together with his rank badge. The latter having a yellow border, a feature worn by all RSMs in the Royal Armoured Corps. **Fig.4c** The yellow embroidered title, worn on the shoulder strap.

No.14 Dress – Shirt sleeve order

Fig.5a Warrant Officer wearing forage cap, WO's regimental pattern, short-sleeved, shirt, stable belt and No.2 Dress trousers. **Fig.5b** Regimental slip-on, worn on this shirt. **Fig.5c** Leather wristlet. These issue items are worn by all WOs, on the right wrist in SSO, this example has a red backing.

Fig.6a Sergeant, with blue beret, green combat shirt, of the pattern introduced c.1988. He is also wearing regimental stable belt and lightweight trousers. **Fig.6b** Regimental slip-on, used on this pattern of shirt. **Fig.6c** Rank wristlet. In temperate areas, rank badges are not worn on shirts, however soldiers often wear SSO during warm weather. While WOs are issued with leather rank wristlets, this is not the case for other NCOs. Thus in some regiments cloth rank wristlets are made by the tailor, usually from whatever is to hand. The example illustrated here, emanated from the Light Dragoons.

Fig.7a Other Ranks' cap badge. When it is worn in the beret, a red felt outline backing is worn behind it, as here. **Fig.7b** Officers' wire embroidered beret badge, Fig.7c Officers' collar badge. **Fig.8** Regimental arm badge, woven with a merrow edge. **Fig.9** WO I rank slide. **Fig.10a** Gold anodised shoulder title, **Fig.10b** Small gilding metal shoulder title, **Fig.10c** Large gilding metal shoulder title. **Fig.11** Squadron flag.

Fig.2a

Fig.2b

Fig.2d

Fig.2c

Fig.3a

Fig.3b

Fig.3c

Fig.3d

Fig.4a

Fig.4b

Fig.4c

Fig.5a

Fig.5b

Fig.6b

Fig.6a

Fig.5c

Fig.6c

Fig.7a

Fig.7b

Fig.7c

Fig.8

Fig.9

Fig.10a

Fig.10b

Fig.10c

Fig.11

QUEEN'S BAYS (2nd Dragoon Guards)

No.1 Dress

Forage Cap – All Ranks wore a blue cap with a white band and welt.

Jacket – Other Ranks had a blue jacket, with shoulder chains. The officers used a similar jacket, but with plain patch breast pockets. Only Other Ranks wore collar badges in No.1 Dress. Chevrons and WOs' badges are gold on white, while the regimental NCOs' arm badge was also embroidered on white. Standard rank badges for Officers wore, with small gilt shoulder titles and buttons on their shoulder chains.

Trousers – All Ranks, blue, with a white stripe, 1¾ inches wide.

No.5 Dress – Battledress

Other Ranks had a white lanyard around their right shoulder, together with the large size gilding metal shoulder titles and collar badges. Officers did not wear lanyards, however, they did wear small size, gilt shoulder strap titles. They usually used their Service Dress cap in battledress, on which was worn a bronze cap badge, with bronze collar badges. Officers wore gilt rank badges, without enamel..

No.6 Dress – Tropical Dress.

Between 1954 and 1957, the Queen's Bays were stationed in Libya and Jordan.**Fig.1a** Shows a trooper, wearing the standard 1950 Pattern issue Khaki Drill uniform. This consisted of an aertex jacket, with permanently attached belt and either Khaki Drill shorts or trousers. Both these fastened at the waist with cross-over straps, attached to buckles at the side of the garment. He has a dark blue beret, with cap badge. **Fig.1b** Cap badge with red backing, for wear on the beret. Officers had a wire embroidered beret badge. **Fig.1c** In warm weather the jacket could be worn as a shirt, tucked into the shorts, or trousers, usually with the issue Pattern 1937 W.E. belt. He also has the matching Khaki Drill bush hat.

No.7 Dress – Mess Dress (Home)

Officers – jacket of scarlet superfine cloth, with a white roll collar. The collar and the white pointed cuffs both trimmed with 1-inch gold lace. The gold cord shoulder straps were fitted with a regimental button and embroidered rank badges. The scarlet vest was edged with ¾-inch gold French braid down the front and along both bottom edges, for three inches each side. Collar badges were not worn.

Fig.2a Other Ranks' gilding metal cap badge, with St Edward's (Queen's) crown. **Fig.2b** Other Ranks Tudor (King's) crown collar badge. **Fig.2c** Metal shoulder title worn by Other Ranks on battledress. **Fig.2b** NCOs' regimental arm badge, without a coloured backing, for Corporals and above. A wire embroidered version, on a white background, was for No.1 and No.3 Dress.

Other Items of Dress

Side hat – white body, with blue flaps and peak and white tip. The Other Ranks' version had no piping and was fitted Universal Pattern (Royal Arms) brass buttons.

Stable belt – red, white, red, in three equal bands, fastened with two nickel plated, single pronged, roller type buckles and brown leather straps. The belt was worn fastened at the front of the wearer, with the strap ends facing the left.

QUEEN'S BAYS (2nd Dragoon Guards)

Fig.1a

Fig.1b

Fig.1c

Fig.2b

Fig.2a

Fig.2c

Fig.2d

QUEEN'S DRAGOON GUARDS

No.1 Dress

Forage Cap – All Ranks wear a blue cap, with a blue velvet band and blue welts.
Jacket – All Ranks, blue, with shoulder chains and fitted with metal shoulder titles. ORs wear issue metal collar badges, while the officers wear a wire embroidered version. Chevrons and WOs' badges are gold on blue, while the regimental NCOs' arm badge is also embroidered on blue. Officers wear standard rank badges.
Trousers – All Ranks, blue, with a white stripe, 1¾ inches wide.

No.2 Dress

Fig.1a Sergeant in 1980 Pattern, No.2 Dress, easily identified by its plain patch breast pockets. A white lanyard on his right arm and ribbons for the Campaign Service Medal (Northern Ireland) and the UN Cyprus Medal. **Fig.1b** Ors' chrome cap badge, **Fig.1c** gold anodised collar badge, **Fig.1d** gold anodised shoulder title. **Fig.1e** insignia on right arm, **Fig.1f** silver anodiesd NCOs' arm badge, with royal blue backing.

Fig.2a Service Dress, used by Colonel CCS Wright, OBE (late QDG). Originally tailored for him in 1958, it is cavalry pattern, made in a heavyweight, light-coloured whipcord material. The ribbons are for the OBE, General Service Medal and the Campaign Service Medal. **Fig.2b** Plain cuff fitted with three regimental buttons. **Fig.2c** Shoulder strap, with rank badges and QDG title. **Fig.3** QDG officers' forage cap.

No.4 Dress

Fig.4a Uniform worn by Colonel TW Muir (late QDG). Made in 1974, it is based on the later cavalry pattern jacket, with the breast pockets having rectangular flaps. **Fig.4b** Ribbons for the 1939-45 Star, Italy Star, Defence Medal, War Medal 1939-45, Campaign Service Medal and the General Service Medal. It should be noted that the last two ribbons have been put on incorrectly, they should be worn in the reverse order. **Fig.4c** QDG button, these are being worn instead of the staff pattern. **Fig.4d** Plain cuff, with two buttons. **Fig.4e** Shoulder strap, with rank badges and QDG title.

No.5 Dress – Desert combat dress.

Fig.4a Trooper in the desert version of Soldier '95, together with the nylon 1958 Pattern belt. **Fig.5b** Union flag and 4th Armoured Brigade formation signs, worn on his left arm. Although a blue, white and blue Tactical Recognition Flash had been approved for wear by the QDG, it does not appear to have been adopted. **Fig.5c** Corporals' rank wristlet. While WOs are given an issue leather wrist strap for their rank badges, NCOs are not. However, in some regiments, such as the QDG, these are also worn by NCOs. **Fig.6** Officers' beret.

Fig.7 Officers' beret badge **Fig.8** Officers' No.1 Dress collar badge **Fig.9** Officers' cloth shoulder title. **Fig.10a** NCOs' arm badge, as worn on No.1 Dress. **Fig.10b** NCOs' arm badge, for Mess Dress, **Fig.10c** NCOs arm badge, for Corporals in Working Dress. **Fig.11** Other Ranks' regimental slides and that worn by Cpl. As Lcpls in the QDG wear two chevrons, Cpls wear the NCOs' arm badge above their two chevrons to fully indicate their rank. **Fig.12** Royal Blue stable belt, with brown leather straps and single pronged, roller type buckles.

QUEEN'S DRAGOON GUARDS

Fig.1a

Fig.1b

Fig.1c

Fig.1d

Fig.1e

Fig.1f

Fig.2a

Fig.3

Fig.2b

Fig.2c

Fig.4a

Fig.4b

Fig.4c

Fig.4d

Fig.4e

Fig.5a

Fig.6

Fig.5b

Fig.5c

Fig.8

Fig.7

Fig.9

Fig.10a

Fig.10b

Fig.10c

Fig.11

Fig.12

QUEEN'S OWN HUSSARS

No.1 Dress

Forage Cap – All Ranks wore a scarlet cap, with scarlet band and welts. Other Ranks used the standard metal cap badge, while officers had a special pattern cap badge in wire embroidery.
Jacket – All Ranks, blue, with shoulder chains. The officers' pattern had a scarlet collar, plain patch breast pockets and shoulder titles on the shoulder straps. Chevrons and WOs' badges were gold on scarlet. The regimental NCOs' arm badge was silver wire embroidered on a Garter Blue backing. Officers used small gilt rank badges, on Garter Blue backings.
Trousers – blue, with a double yellow stripe, ¾ inches wide and $^1/_8$ inch apart.

Fig.1a No.1 Dress, worn by Major MJ Filby, MC, who was originally commissioned during the Second World War, serving with the 3rd Hussars. With the introduction of No.1 Dress, in the late 1940s, he had this uniform made for him. When the regiment amalgamated with the 7th Hussars, in 1958, to form the Queen's Own Hussars, he was fortunate in that the pattern adopted was almost identical to that used by the 3rd Hussars. The only difference being that the 3rd Hussars had three cuff buttons, while the QOH only had two. Other than that, all he had to do was simply change the collar badges and shoulder titles to the new pattern. **Fig.1b** Medal ribbons for the Military Cross (notified in the London Gazette 6.6.46), 1939-45 Star, Burma Star, Defence Medal, War Medal 1939-45 with Mentioned in Despatches (notified in the London Gazette 9.5.46) General Service Medal (the 3rd Hussars served in Palestine) Coronation Medal of 1953 and the Territorial Efficiency Medal. The latter may have been awarded for his pre-war TA service. **Fig.1c** Shoulder chain, note the small gilt metal crown on the Garter Blue backing and also the metal shoulder title. **Fig.1d** Plain pointed cuff, with two inch opening, closed with three buttons. It should be noted that officers of the 3rd Hussars, 7th Hussars and QOH all wore plain, full dome, gilt burnished buttons, in all orders of dress except Mess Dress. This photo also illustrates the overalls, with their double yellow stripes.

No.2 Dress

Fig.2a Shows a WO II in one of the early patterns of No.2 Dress, easily recognised by its box pleated breast pockets. This pattern superseded the 1964 Pattern, but unfortunately was not given a pattern designation. It is fitted with gold anodised, plain domed buttons. **Fig.2b** Medal ribbons for the British Empire Medal, General Service Medal (Northern Ireland) UN Cyprus Medal, Meritorious Service Medal and the Army Long Service and Good Conduct Medal. Above the ribbons are thread loops for the attachment of his full-size medals, which are mounted on a pin back bar. Also it still retains the trouser band hook, fitted above the ribbons. This was a temporary measure, used when medals were actually being presented. **Fig.2c** Issue gold and silver collar badge, mounted on a red felt backing. These backings are held in place by the collar badges themselves. **Fig.2d** Gold anodised shoulder title, worn on both shoulder straps. **Fig.2e** Lower right arm with gold anodised rank badge and chrome NCOs' arm badge, both of which have Garter Blue backings. These are sewn to the uniform and not held in place with the badges. **Fig.2f** Lower left arm, gold anodised rank badge on backing and also the Maid of Warsaw regimental arm badge. This was originally awarded to the 7th Queen's Own Hussars by the Commander of the Second Polish Corps in Italy, in recognition of their support during the Second World War. Other Ranks wear a white embroidered version on the red shield

QUEEN'S OWN HUSSARS

Fig.1a

Fig.1b

Fig.1c

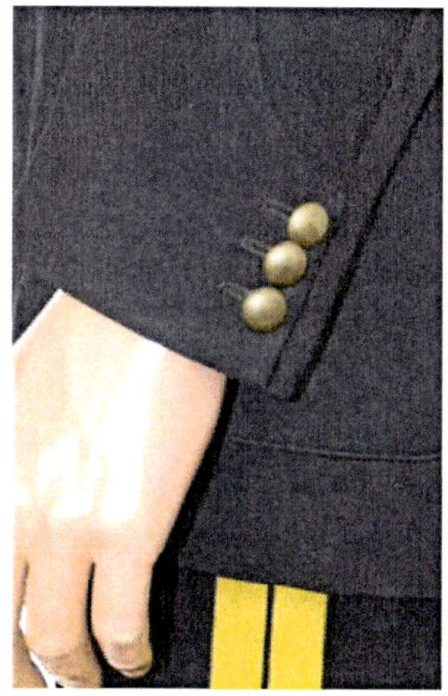

Fig.1d

Fig.2a

Fig.2b

Fig.2c

Fig.2d

Fig.2e

Fig.2f

Fig.3a Service Dress uniform worn by Capt. MWT Price. It is of the cavalry pattern, with plain patch breast pockets and jetted side pockets, both with rectangular flaps. Originally made for him in 1963, from a medium khaki cavalry twill. It is being worn here with his Service Dress cap, which has the standard cap badge. **Fig.3b** Officers' pattern collar badge, made from silver, gilt and blue enamel. Unlike the Other Ranks, it is worn without the scarlet backing on Service Dress. **Fig.3c** Lower left cuff, note the Maid of Warsaw badge. Officers wore a silver wire embroidered version on the scarlet shield. The cuffs are plain, with a two inch opening, fastened with two plain gilt buttons. **Fig.3d** Shoulder strap fitted with small gilt rank stars, on Garter Blue backings and with metal shoulder titles.

Fig.4a Cap badge. **Fig.4b** Special pattern of cap badge for an officers' forage cap, coloured side hat and beret. The standard pattern was worn in their Service Dress cap. **Fig.5a** Majors' rank slide **Fig.5b** Cloth shoulder title for officers in battledress. Other Ranks used metal shoulder titles. **Fig.6** sSable belt.

No.10 Dress – Temperate Mess Dress

Other Ranks – 1902 Pattern jacket, in dark blue barathea, with a stand collar and an open front, fastened with a gold gimp loop at the base of the collar. Collar is scarlet and is also trimmed at the top, bottom and front with gold gimp. It has gold twisted shoulder cords, which fasten with small regimental buttons. The cuffs are finished plain, with gold gimp Austrian knots. There are no buttons down the front of the jacket, which is trimmed with gold gimp. Collar and rank badges, also chevrons are similar to those worn on No.1 Dress. A Garter Blue cummerbund, six inches wide, with No.1 Dress trousers, completes this order.

Officers – 1902 Pattern jacket, dark blue, with a scarlet collar, which fastens with two hooks and a loop. The front, top and bottom of the collar are edged with ¾-in gold lace. The back of the collar is decorated with No.9 gold Russia gimp. The front, bottom and back of the jacket are edged with gold lace ¾-in wide. The shoulder cords are constructed from Navy Blue mohair and the rank badges are embroidered in silver wire. The plain cuffs are decorated with a crows' foot in gold Russia gimp. The Mess Vest is of scarlet cloth, the collar being trimmed with No.4 gold Russia gimp. The front is fastened with hooks and eyes and the two bottom pockets are also trimmed with gold Russia gimp. The vest is worn with a white strip collar, fitted to the inside of the collar, so that it is visible for $^1/_8$–in above the collar and with a ¼-in gap either side of the front centre.

No.11 Dress – Tropical Mess Dress

Other Ranks – 1902 Pattern, in white drill material, with a stand collar, fastened with two hooks and eyes, the jacket open at the front. The shoulder straps, collar and pointed cuffs are made from white drill. Collar badges, rank badges and chevrons are similar to those on No.1 Dress. This is also worn with the Garter Blue cummerbund, identical to that worn with No.10 Dress.

Other Items of Dress

Side hat – scarlet body and flaps, all edged with gold gimp and scarlet tip. Other Ranks used the standard metal cap badge, while Officers wore the special embroidered pattern of badge.

Fig.3a

Fig.3b

Fig.3c

Fig.3d

Fig.4b

Fig.4a

Fig.5

Fig.6a

Fig.6b

Fig.7

QUEEN'S ROYAL HUSSARS

No.1 Dress

Forage Cap – All Ranks wear a scarlet cap, with scarlet band and welts. All officers have ¾-inch gold braid on the peaks of their caps, irrespective of rank.

Jacket – All Ranks, blue, with a scarlet collar and shoulder chains. Chevrons and WOs' badges are gold on scarlet, the chevrons having a shamrock design on them. The regimental NCOs' arm badge is wire embroidered, on a Garter Blue backing. Rank badges for Officers are small gilt, on Garter Blue backings.

Trousers – blue, with a double yellow stripe, ¾ inches wide and $^1/_8$ inch apart.

No.2 Dress – Service Dress

Fig.1a Officer in cavalry pattern Service Dress, of drab khaki whipcord. He is wearing the tent hat, previously worn by the Queen's Royal Irish Hussars, who had in turn inherited it from the 8th King's Royal Irish Hussars. Note the white shirt, which has box pleated breast pockets and shoulder straps and the khaki tie. On his lower left arm, the wire embroidered Maid of Warsaw arm badge can also be seen. **Fig.1b** Collar badge. The white Horse of Hanover was previously worn on the cap badge of the Queen's Own Hussars and, before that, the 3rd King's Own Hussars. **Fig.1c** Shoulder strap, showing title and rank stars. These small rank stars, with their Garter Blue backings, were previously worn by the QOH. **Fig.1d** Rank star. This pattern with screw fitting is normally worn on shoulder chains, although fitted in this case to Service Dress.

Fig.2a Cap badge **Fig.2b** Officers' forage cap badge **Fig.2c** Officers' beret badge. **Fig.3a** Other Ranks' Maid of Warsaw badge, the Officers version having silver wire embroidery. **Fig.3b** NCOs' arm badge. This embroidered version is worn on No.1 Dress and Mess Dress. A metal version, on a Garter Blue backing, is worn on No.2 Dress. **Fig.3c** Lt-Cols' rank slide.

No.10 Dress – Temperate Mess Dress

Other Ranks – dark blue superfine material, with a scarlet stand collar, decorated with shamrock lace. The plain, blue cuffs have Russia lace loops on them. There are no shoulder straps on the jacket, which is also devoid of collar badges and buttons. Badges of rank are $^2/_3{}^{rd}$ size, the chevrons again being made from shamrock pattern lace. The vest is also scarlet, with a stand collar and a single line of gold cord down the front. There are two pockets and the vest is also devoid of buttons. A cummerbund is not worn.

Other Items of Dress

Beret – A Rifle Green beret, with a green ribbon band, is worn with a metal cap badge by ORs and an embroidered badge by Officers. This is identical to the pattern previously worn by the Queen's Royal Irish Hussars.

Regimental pullover – dark green in colour, ribbed knit with a round neck. The dark green epaulettes are embroidered with the regimental title and are fastened with leather buttons. It also has green elbow patches. This pattern is worn by Senior NCOs and WOs.

Side hat – None for Other Ranks, although the officers continue to wear the 8th King's Royal Irish Hussars/QRIH pattern of tent hat.

Stable belt – Garter Blue 20mm, yellow 3mm, green 25mm, yellow, 3mm and Garter Blue 20mm. It is fitted with stirrup shaped buckles, fastening with two brown leather straps.

QUEEN'S ROYAL HUSSARS

Fig.1a

Fig.1d

Fig.1b

Fig.1c

Fig.2a

Fig.2b

Fig.2c

Fig.3a

Fig.3b

Fig.3c

QUEEN'S ROYAL IRISH HUSSARS

No.1 Dress

Forage Cap – All Ranks wore a red cap, with red band and welts. Other Ranks used a metal cap badge, while officers had an embroidered badge. Officers also wore the tent hat, with this order of dress, on non-ceremonial occassions.

Jacket – All Ranks, blue, with shoulder chains and collar badges. Chevrons and WOs' badges are gold on scarlet, the chevrons being of shamrock lace. Good conduct chevrons have gold shamrock lace on a dark blue backing. The regimental NCOs' arm badge is metal. Officers wear standard rank badges.

Trousers – blue, with a double yellow stripe, ¾ inches wide and $^{1}/_{8}$ inch apart.

No.2 Dress – Service Dress

Fig.1a Uniform worn by Captain EJD Martin, 1983. This can be worn either with the coloured forage cap, khaki Service Dress hat, or tent hat, as here. This uniform is of the cavalry pattern, in drab khaki whipcord, with plain patch breast pockets and inset side pockets, all with rectangular flaps. It has plain gilt buttons, those down the front are full ball type, while the remainder are half ball buttons. **Fig.1b** Collar with Officers' silver and gilt collar badge. **Fig.1c** Rank badges, these consist of a combination of cloth and wire embroidery.

Fig.2 Other Ranks' forage cap. In No.2 Dress, a yellow lanyard around the right shoulder and gold anodised shoulder titles. LCpls in this regiment wore two chevrons, while Cpls wore two chevrons with the regimental pattern NCOs' arm badge above them. The side hat was worn on informal occasions.

No.3 Dress – Warm weather ceremonial uniform

The QRIH were stationed in Cyprus, at various times during the 1970s and 1980s, as part of the United Nations peacekeeping force. Their final deployment there was in 1993, just prior to amalgamation. **Fig.3a** Lt wearing No.3 Dress, whilst serving with the UN in Cyprus. This is effectively a lightweight white version of No.1 Dress, for wear in warm and hot climates. Of note are the collar badges worn on this particular uniform, which are the Other Ranks' anodised type. They are not the more expensive silver and gilt version, that were worn on the Service Dress, see Fig.1b. This may be because the officer was on a three year Short Service Commission or, with amalgamation imminent, he had decided not to incur the extra expense. All troops serving with the UN wear the blue UN beret, instead of their own regimental headdress. **Fig.3b** Insignia worn on left arm. The shoulder chains are fitted with the small plain gilt rank stars. The full ball buttons down the front of his jacket can clearly be seen.. See Figs.3c and 5c for full descriptions of the other badges. **Fig.3c** United Nations badge, worn by all troops serving with the UN. Below this is the Union Flag, worn by British troops to identify their country of origin. **Fig.4a** Is the Other Ranks' UN cap badge, also worn by some officers. **Fig.4b** Embroidered UN cap badge, usually purchased and worn by Officers.

No.4 Dress – Warm weather service dress.

Fig.5a No.4 Dress uniform, belonging to the same officer shown in Fig.3a above, whilst serving in Cyprus. This is the lightweight version of No.2 Dress, worn only by officers, in warm and hot climates. However, on closer examination, it should be noted that the breast pockets on this uniform have pointed flaps, whilst the Service Dress uniform in Fig.1a have rectangular flaps. **Fig.5b** Rank badges, these consist of a combination of cloth and wire embroidery. They are identical to those worn on Service Dress.

QUEEN'S ROYAL IRISH HUSSARS

Fig.2

Fig.1a

Fig.1b

Fig.1c

Fig.4a

Fig.4b

Fig.3a

Fig.3b

Fig.3c

Fig.5c Duke of Edinburgh's arm badge. This special embellishment was inaugurated in 1958, when the QRIH were formed. The Colonel-in-Chief of the new regiment, HRH Prince Philip, Duke of Edinburgh, gave approval for an annual competition. This took place annually, from one Balaclava Day to the next and covered training, sport and administration. The winning Squadron were awarded the Duke of Edinburgh's cipher, which was worn on their left forearm. Due to deployments and a change in the unit's role during the 1970s, it became impossible to continue with the various competitions. In the late 1970s this honour was conferred on 'A' Squadron, being the senior squadron. The badge worn by Other Ranks consists of yellow embroidery on a dark blue oval. **Fig.5d** Shows the positioning of the various insignia worn on the left arm. Again note the full ball buttons worn on the front of the jacket.

Fig.6a Crewman's arm badge and **Fig.6b** Tank commander's arm badge. Both of these badges were introduced for wear in combat dress about 1990. **Fig.7a** Anodised shoulder title worn by Other Ranks in No.2 Dress. **Fig.7b** Anodised NCOs' arm badge, for Cpls and above, in No.1 and No.2 Dress. **Fig.8a** Other Ranks' Rifle Green beret, with green ribbon band and metal cap badge. **Fig.8b** Officers' embroidered cap badge for red forage cap. **Fig.9** Stable belt, three inches wide.

No.10 Dress – Temperate Mess Dress

Other Ranks – 1939 pattern, black cloth jacket, with a roll collar faced in emerald green, ribbed silk. It is devoid of shoulder straps and buttons. The plain cuffs and backseams were embellished with *gutless braid*, $^5/_{16}$ inches wide. The jacket fastened with a *job-chain*. Collar badges were worn, together with rank badges, similar to those worn on No.1 Dress. A special pattern of NCOs' arm badge was also used. The cummerbund was five inches wide and yellow/gold in colour.

Officer – 1902 pattern, dark blue jacket with a stand collar, trimmed along the top and front edges with ¾ inch shamrock lace, while the bottom edge is trimmed with gold gimp. Collar badges are not worn. The front and bottom edges of the jacket are also trimmed in this gold braid. The shoulder straps are constructed from black gimp cord, on which $^3/_8$ inch size, silver embroidered rank badges are placed. The rear side seams are decorated in black gimp cord, with crows' feet ends. The cuffs are also trimmed in black gimp cord, forming a hussar ring on each sleeve. Finally the jacket is fitted with four olivettes down the left front. The 1902 pattern vest is green, with a stand collar. The edges and part of the collar are trimmed with gold Russia braid. The side pockets are also trimmed with gold Russia braid, the ends of which terminate in crows' feet.

Other Items of Dress

Beret – When the regiment was formed, in 1958, the standard issue dark blue beret was authorised. Not long after, a dark green ribbon band, ¾ inches wide was added to it. This not only gave it a distinctive look, similar to that worn by the 11th Hussars, but also reinforced their Irish link. This was worn for a fairly long time, although in use the band soiled and became less obviously coloured. In about 1983 the regiment were permitted to adopt the Rifle Green beret, to which the ribbon band was attached. Examples examined have a $^7/_8$ inch wide band. This more distinctive form of headdress was worn up until their amalgamation in 1993.
Side hat – Officers wore the distinctive tent hat. Other Ranks wore a similar type of hat, but with yellow worsted braid and piping and a metal cap badge.

Fig.5b

Fig.5a

Fig.5c

Fig.5d

Fig.6a

Fig.7a

Fig.8a

Fig.6b

Fig.7b

Fig.8b

Fig.9

QUEEN'S ROYAL LANCERS

No.1 Dress

Forage Cap – All Ranks wear a scarlet cap, with a blue band. It also has a blue welt around the crown and blue quarter welts and was previously worn by the 16th/5th Lancers. All Ranks had a metal cap badge.
Jacket – All Ranks, blue, with shoulder chains. Other Ranks have white gorget patches, fitted with silver anodised collar badges. Officers do not wear gorgets, but instead have silver and gilt collar badges. Chevrons and WOs' badges are gold on white. Officers used standard rank badges.
Trousers – All Ranks, blue, with double white stripes ¾ inch wide and ¼ inch apart.

No.2 Dress

Fig.1a Trooper in 1980 Pattern, No.2 Dress, easily identified by the plain patch breast pockets. Lanyards are not worn by the QRL.. **Fig.1b** Cap badge, previously worn by the 17th/21st Lancers. **Fig.1c** Other Ranks' silver anodised collar badge, previously worn by the 16th/5th Lancers. Officers wear a similar pattern, but in gilt and silver. **Fig.1d** ORs' shoulder title, Officers with bronze shoulder titles. **Fig.2** 21st Lancers' arm badge. This has, at times, been worn by All Ranks in No.1 Dress, No.2 Dress and Mess Dress.

No.10 Dress – Temperate Mess Dress

Other Ranks – The scarlet jacket has a dark blue collar, and cuffs. The front, collar and edge of the blue cuffs are trimmed in flat gold braid. The collar has embroidered collar badges, of the 16th/5th Lancers' pattern. The ivory white Vest, has a stand collar. The collar and front of the vest is edged with 12.7mm gold braid. The vest fastens at the front, a zip fastener being concealed behind the gold braiding. Pockets, piped in gold, are fitted to either side of the vest.
Officers – The scarlet jacket has a blue stand collar. The collar and front of the jacket are both trimmed in 1 inch wide gold, scalloped edge, lace. The seams on the back of the jacket, together with those on the back of the sleeves, are piped in dark blue. The dark blue, pointed cuffs are trimmed in 1 inch goold lace. The jacket fastens at the collar, with a gold Russia loop, collar badges are not worn. The double gimp shoulder cords are secured with a regimental button and are fitted with silver wire embroidered badges of rank. The white ivory vest has a stand collar and is decorated extensively with gold braid.

Fig.3a Tactical Recognition Flash (TRF) and **Fig.3b** TRF, as worn on Desert DPM clothing. **Fig.4** On the issue dark blue beret, the cap badge is worn on a scarlet felt backing. **Fig.5a** Staff Sergeants' rank slide. **Fig.5b** Majors' rank slide, as worn on Desert DPM uniform. **Fig.6** Sergeants' Mess Dress arm badge, worn on the chevrons.

Other Items of Dress

Regimental pullover – WOs and Senior NCOs wear a knit of grey, blue and green, lightly ribbed and with a round neck. It has green suede epaulettes, which have brown leather buttons and gun metal titles. The pullover also has green suede elbow patches, which end 50.8mm from the cuff.

Stable belt – The original pattern consisted of scarlet, 25% wide, blue, white, blue white totalling 50% and scarlet 25%. This was fitted with a chrome metal plate, with the regimental 'motto' badge. In 1998 this was superseded with a scarlet, white, scarlet, white and scarlet belt, fitted with two single pronged, roller type buckles and brown leather straps.

QUEEN'S ROYAL LANCERS

Fig.1a

Fig.1b

Fig.2

Fig.1c

Fig.1d

Fig.3a

Fig.4

Fig.3b

Fig.5a

Fig.6

Fig.5b

ROYAL ARMOURED CORPS

The Royal Armoured Corps is an administrative and training body only, with its uniform and insignia being worn only by staff and recruits.

No.1 Dress
Forage Cap – All Ranks wear a red cap, with a red welt around the crown. It also has a yellow band, with black welts at both top and bottom.
Jacket – All Ranks, blue, with shoulder chains. Officers wore standard rank badges.
Trousers – All Ranks, blue, with a single yellow stripe 1¾ inch wide.

No.5 Dress – Battledress
Fig.1a Major in the standard 1949 Pattern battledress and Service Dress hat. **Fig.1b** Layout of badges and insignia, showing the red on yellow shoulder titles and his yellow backed rank badges. **Fig.1c** Ribbons for the 1939-45 Star, Africa Star with 8th Army clasp, France and Germany Star, Defence Medal and the War Medal 1939-45. **Fig.1d** RAC Training Brigade formation sign, consisting of a mailed fist with the Torch of Learning.

Fig.2 Forage cap **Fig.3a** Other Ranks' collar badge, which are identical to the cap badge, only smaller. **Fig.3b** Officers' collar badge for Service Dress. **Fig.4** Gilding metal shoulder title, for wear on tropical uniforms.

In 1949 the War Office introduced a special arm badge, to be worn by all ranks of the Royal Armoured Corps (including the RTR). It was intended to create a cohesiveness amongst all units of the RAC, similar to the regimental arm badges. It was about the size of the collar badge, worn on the left upper arm of the battledress blouse, immediately below the formation badge, or immediately above the rank chevrons of NCOs. It was never a popular badge, many regiments totally ignoring it, with the result that it disappeared in the mid-1950s. **Fig.5a** The yellow on khaki version, of the RAC arm badge, for battledress. **Fig.5d** The wire version, of the RAC arm badge, for No.1 Dress, which is smaller than the version worn on battledress.

Other Items of Dress
Fig.6 Stable belt. Although this is identical in colour to that worn by the 9th Queen's Royal Lancers, there are two distinct differences. Firstly the straps on the RAC stable belt are made from black leather, whilst those on the 9th Lancers stable belt are brown. Secondly, it has a nickel plated, slide adjuster, while that worn by the 9th Lancers has none.

ROYAL ARMOURED CORPS

Fig.1c

Fig.1d

Fig.1a

Fig.1b

Fig.3a

Fig.2

Fig.5a

Fig.3b

Fig.4

Fig.5b

Fig.6

ROYAL DRAGOON GUARDS

No.1 Dress

Forage Cap – All Ranks, blue, with a Royal Blue band and Royal Blue welt around the crown. This was previously worn by the 4th/7th Royal Dragoon Guards. All officers have ¾-inch gold braid on the peaks of their caps, irrespective of rank.
Jacket – All Ranks, blue, with shoulder chains. Chevrons and WOs' badges are gold on Royal Blue. On their right arm, Sergeants and WOs have a metal White Horse of Hanover, on a green felt backing. This was previously worn by the 5th Royal Inniskilling Dragoon Guards. On their lower left arm, Sergeants and WOs also wear a wire embroidered regimental arm badge. Officers used standard rank badges.
Trousers – All Ranks, green, with a 1¾-in wide primrose stripe.

No.2 Dress

Fig.1a Lcpl in 1980 pattern No.2 Dress uniform, easily identified by the plain patch breast pockets. The RDG wear plain green trousers with this order of dress, identical to those previously worn by the 5th Royal Inniskilling Dragoon Guards. **Fig.1b** Rear view of the pouch belt. **Fig.1c** Insignia on left arm. **Fig.1d** Other Ranks' gold anodised shoulder title. **Fig.1e** Regimental arm badge, worn by all ranks on their upper left arm. This was previously worn by the 4th/7th Royal Dragoon Guards. **Fig.1f** White Horse of Hanover, for Sgts and S/Sgts on the right arm chevrons., on a green felt backing. WOs place this below their rank badge. **Fig.1g** Other Ranks' pouch belt.

No.5 Dress – Desert combat dress.

Fig.2a Trooper wearing the desert DPM field jacket, which is similar to the standard DPM version, with slotted buttons and rank slide on the front. **Fig.2b** Insignia on the right arm, in this case the RDG TRF. **Fig.2c** Insignia on left arm. This consists of the Union flag, below which is the 4th Armoured Brigade formation sign. The field jacket can be worn with a detachable, wired hood, as here. **Fig.2d** Name tape above left breast pocket, written in both English and Arabic.

No.10 Dress – Temperate Mess Dress

Fig.3a Lcpl in Other Ranks' pattern Mess Dress. The jacket is scarlet, with Royal Blue collar and pointed cuffs. Collar badges are normally worn, but there is no evidence of them having been worn on this jacket. The 'U' shaped, Royal Blue Mess Vest has five small regimental buttons. **Fig.3b** Single chevron, worn by the Lcpl, of gold shamrock lace on a Royal Blue backing. **Fig.3c** Shoulder straps trimmed with gold braid. **Fig.3d** Blue pointed cuff and green trousers, which have a 1¾-in wide primrose stripe. **Fig.3e** NATO Kosovo Medal, this miniature medal being worn on the left lapel.

Fig.4a Other Ranks' silver anodised cap badge. **Fig.4b** All Ranks' cap badge, which replaced the previous version. Collar badges were similar to this, only smaller. **Fig.5a** ORs' cloth beret badge, used before metal badges were available. **Fig.5b** Small anodised beret badge, worn by Senior NCOs and WOs. Similar to the collar badge, it instead has a cap badge slider fitting. **Fig.5c** ORs metal cap badge, for wear on the beret. When worn on the blue beret, all metal badges have a loose maroon backing added to them. **Fig.5d** Officers' wire embroidered beret badge. **Fig.6** Tactical Recognition Flash. **Fig.7a** S/Sgt rank slide and **Fig.7b** SQMS rank slide.

ROYAL DRAGOON GUARDS

Fig.1d

Fig.1a

Fig.1b

Fig.1c

Fig.1f

Fig.1e

Fig.1g

Fig.2a

Fig.2b

Fig.2c

Fig.2d

Fig.3a

Fig.3b

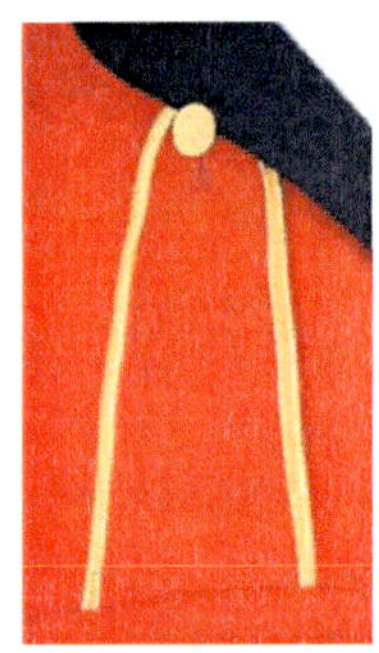
Fig.3c

Fig.3d

Fig.3e

Fig.4a

Fig.4b

Fig.5a

Fig.5b

Fig.5c

Fig.5d

Fig.7a

Fig.6

Fig.7b

1st ROYAL DRAGOONS

No.1 Dress
Forage Cap – All Ranks wore the standard infantry 'Royal' pattern, which is blue, with scarlet band and welt around the crown. Other Ranks used the issue metal cap badge, whilst officers had a gold embroidered cap badge.
Jacket – All Ranks, blue, with shoulder chains and collar badges. Chevrons and WOs' badges were gold on blue, together with an embroidered NCOs' arm badge. Officers used standard badges of rank.
Trousers – All Ranks, blue, with a single yellow stripe 1¾ inch wide.

Fig.1a Other Ranks' bi-metal cap badge, later superseded by a gold and silver anodised version. **Fig.1b** Officers' forage cap, with gold embroidered cap badge. **Fig.1c** Officers' bronze cap badge, which is smaller than the ORs' cap badge and was for the khaki Service Dress cap.

Not only were the collar badges identical in design to the cap badge, but they were also the same size as the Officers' bronze cap badge illustrated here. ORs had bi-metal collar badges and later a similar anodised version. Officers wore silver and gilt collar badges on No1 Dress and bronze collar badges on No.2 Service Dress.

Fig.2a The Tudor crown version of the NCOs' metal arm badge, with black backing, worn on Battledress. **Fig.2b** The St Edward's crown version of the NCOs metal arm badge, with black backing, also for Battledress. Wire embroidered versions of these badges were used on No.1 Dress. **Fig.2c** Embroidered NCOs' arm badge, used on No.2 Dress, c.1960-69. **Fig.2d** Lcpls' brass chevron, with black backing, for use on working dress. Officers also had black backings to their Service Dress rank badges..

Fig.3a Gilding metal shoulder title. **Fig.3b** Gold anodised shoulder title, Other Ranks on No.2 Dress. **Fig.3c** Embroidered shoulder title for Officers.

No.10 Dress – Temperate Mess Dress
Other Ranks – scarlet 1902 Pattern jacket, with a dark blue stand collar and pointed cuffs. The single twisted, black shoulder cords were fitted with small regimental buttons. The jacket had regimental collar badges and NCOs arm badges. Rank badges and chevrons were similar to those worn on No.1 Dress, but smaller. The dark blue Mess Vest was triangular in shape, fastening with straps at the neck and back. A cummerbund was not worn.

No.11 Dress – Tropical Mess Dress
Other Ranks – white drill, 1939 pattern jacket, with roll collar and pointed cuffs. The jacket had white drill shoulder straps, which fastened with a small regimental button. The front of the jacket was fastened with two linked regimental buttons. Collar badges and rank badges were identical to those worn on No.10 Dress. This was worn with a black, art silk cummerbund, 5½ inches wide.

1st ROYAL DRAGOONS

Fig.1a

Fig.1b

Fig.1c

Fig.2a

Fig.2b

Fig.2c

Fig.2d

Fig.3a

Fig.3b

Fig.3c

ROYAL HUSSARS

No.1 Dress

Forage Cap All Ranks wore a crimson cap, with a crimson welt around the crown. All officers had ¾- inch gold braid on the peaks of their caps, irrespective of rank.
Jacket – All Ranks, blue, with shoulder chains and collar badges. Chevrons and WOs' badges were gold on crimson , the metal NCOs' arm badge was worn on a crimson backing.. Officers wore standard rank badges.
Trousers – Other Ranks, crimson, without stripes. Officers, crimson, with ¾-in wide double yellow stripes, ½-in apart.

Fig.1a Lcpl in No.1 Dress. The medal ribbons above his left breast pocket are for the Campaign Service Medal (N Ireland) and the Gulf Medal of 1992. **Fig.1b** Insignia on his right arm, including single gold on crimson rank chevron and NCOs' arm badge. **Fig.1c** Other Ranks' cap badge. This is similar to the pattern previously worn by the 10th Royal Hussars, with the latter's title changing to The Royal Hussars. **Fig.1d** Other Ranks' collar badge, identical to that previously worn by the 10th Royal Hussars.

Fig.2a Wire embroidered NCOs' arm badge, for Mess Dress. **Fig.2b** Metal NCOs' arm badge for No.1 and No.2 Dress.

No.2 Dress

Other Ranks – issue pattern of khaki jacket, with metal shoulder titles. Collar badges and lanyard were not worn. This was worn with crimson trousers and a crimson forage cap.

Officers – khaki whipcord, cavalry pattern jacket, with plain patch breast pockets and three-point flaps. The side pockets were inset and had rectangular flaps. Shoulder titles were worn, but not collar badges or a lanyard. Rank badges were of the standard pattern, without enamel. The Sam Browne belt was of cavalry pattern, having circular sword rings, while the cross strap was fitted with a whistle. Crimson trousers were worn and either a crimson forage cap, a khaki Service Dress cap, or a crimson side hat, depending upon the occasion. **Fig.3a** Major in Service Dress. **Fig.3b** Pointed cuff, with two inset buttons. **Fig.3c** Shoulder strap, with regimental title and plain anodised rank crown. **Fig.3d** Flat, regimental button. **Fig.3e** Gold anodised shoulder title, for all ranks in No.2 Dress.

No.10 Dress – Temperate Mess Dress

Other Ranks – the navy blue jacket was made from ribbed covered serge with a claret coloured, roll collar. The front was plain, without buttons, and it did not have shoulder straps. The blue pointed cuffs were 6 inches deep at the point and 2½-inches deep at the side. Collar badges were worn, while the rank badges and chevrons were similar to those worn on No.1 Dress. The Mess Vest was navy blue in colour, with a V-front, the roll collar also of V-front style. The vest had welted pockets on either side, in the lower position. It fastened at the front with four small regimental buttons. A cummerbund was not worn.

ROYAL HUSSARS

Fig.1c

Fig.1d

Fig.1a

Fig.1b

Fig.2a

Fig.2b

No.10 Dress – Temperate Mess Dress

Officers – 1902 Pattern jacket, made from dark blue doeskin cloth. The crimson barathea, stand collar was edged with gold lace, along the top and front opening. The base of the collar, together with the front opening and bottom of the jacket were trimmed with ¼-inch gold basket cord. The jacket was further decorated with a single row of No.4 Russia gimp, ½-inch inside the gold lace, down the front and bottom edges. A loop of No.4 Russia braid is attached to the base of the collar on the right, which fastened to a hook on the left side. Collar badges were not worn. The narrow dark blue shoulder straps were decorated with three rows of No.9 gold Russia braid, sewn edge to edge. Silver embroidered rank badges, of $^{5}/_{8}$-inch size, were worn. The 1902 Mess Vest is made from crimson barathea cloth, with a stand collar. It is trimmed with No.4 gold Russia braid along the top and front edge of the collar, continued half way round the front base of the collar. The front of the jacket and the lower edge of each front were also trimmed in No.4 gold Russia braid. The vest has two lower pockets, decorated with No.4 gold Russia braid, with crows' feet at each end of the pocket.

No.11 Dress – Tropical Mess Dress

Other Ranks – 1939 Pattern jacket, in white drill material, with a roll collar and pointed cuffs of the same material. Two small regimental buttons on each cuff, but no other buttons. Collar badges were worn, with a smaller version of the rank badges and chevrons used on No.1 Dress. This was worn with a crimson cummerbund, 4½ inches wide, with three pleats and fastened with two cloth straps and buckles.

Officers – like the ORs' version, this was in white drill material. It had white drill cuffs and shoulder straps, the latter had detachable regimental buttons. There were no buttons on the front, or cuffs. Gold badges of rank were used on the shoulder straps and the order was completed with a crimson cummerbund.

Other Items of Dress

Beret – The Royal Hussars adopted a distinctive brown beret, but constructed as the standard pattern of beret, rather than as the previous 11th Hussars pattern. The crimson band of the 11th Hussars, was replaced with a domed, crimson badge backing. This was added by the regimental tailor, as the berets were supplied without these.
Fig.4 Other Ranks' beret.

Fig.5 Stable belt.

Side hat – Officers, crimson body, piped in gold, with scarlet flaps piped gold and a scarlet peak and tip. Warrant Officers and Sergeants used a similar version, but without the gold piping around the top of the body. It was fitted with two regimental buttons and cap badge. Corporals and below had a similar version to WOs and Sergeants, but without any gold piping.

Tent hat – crimson, embellished with universal gold lace, 1 inch wide and gold gimp $^{3}/_{20}$-inch wide, similar to that worn by the Queen's Royal Irish Hussars. Like the QRIH tent hat, no cap badge was worn.

Fig.3a

Fig.3d

Fig.3e

Fig.3b

Fig.3c

Fig.4

Fig.5

ROYAL SCOTS DRAGOON GUARDS

No.1 Dress

Forage Cap – All Ranks, blue, with a yellow vandyke band and a yellow welt around the crown. The metal cap badge ad a black felt backing.

Jacket – All Ranks, blue, with shoulder chains and collar badges. All Ranks wear an embroidered regimental badge, placed on the upper left arm and consisting of the Prince of Wales's plumes. Chevrons are gold thistle lace, on a yellow backing. WOs' badges and the NCOs' arm badge are also gold embroidered on yellow. Officers wear, uniqueally, embroidered badges of rank on their shoulder chains.

Trousers – All Ranks, blue, with double yellow stripes 1 inch wide and ¼-inch apart.

No.2 Dress

Fig.1a Corporal in 1962 Pattern No.2 Dress. The early patterns of No.2 Dress are easily identified by their box pleated breast pockets. He is wearing the ribbons for the UN Cyprus Medal and Campaign Service Medal, probably for service in Northern Ireland. The cap and collar badges have black felt backings, held in place by the badges. **Fig.1b** Insignia on right arm, the NCOs' arm badge having a black backing. **Fig.1c** Insignia worn on left arm, with a white lanyard and embroidered regimental arm badge. **Fig.1d** Early pattern shoulder title, worn up until about 1981.

Fig.2a WO II in 1980 Pattern No.2 Dress, easily identified by its plain patch breast pockets. The black badge backings, behind the collar badges and NCOs' arm badge, are sewn to the uniform, not held in place by the insignia. The ribbons are for the Campaign Service Medal and the Army Long Service and Good Conduct Medal. **Fig.2b** Rear view showing pouch and badge. **Fig.2c** Left arm insignia and new shoulder title. **Fig.2d** Gold anodised shoulder title, introduced about 1981.

Fig.3a Lt. in Service Dress of khaki whipcord, following the cavalry pattern with plain patch breast pockets. The jacket is fitted with leather 'football' type buttons, as opposed to the normal metal regimental type. The Service Dress cap is unique in having black piping round the crown. A white shirt and light khaki tie are used in this order of dress. The trousers are made from the whipcord, with turn-ups. **Fig.3b** Cloth rank badges, embroidered on khaki, are worn on the shoulder straps. **Fig.3c** At the top of the left arm are the Prince of Wales's plumes, embroidered in wire on a dark blue backing. The cuffs are plain, with a slit at the back, closed with two small leather buttons.

No.10 Dress – Temperate Mess Dress

Officers – 1902 Pattern jacket, scarlet with yellow velvet collar and cuffs. The stand collar has embroidered collar badges. The collar, cuffs and front edges of the jacket are decorated with 1-inch wide, gold thistle lace. The gold twisted shoulder cords are fitted with a regimental button and small embroidered badges of rank. The yellow, 1902 Pattern Vest is trimmed down the front with ¾-inch gold lace. The corners of the vest have small embroidered thistles, in green and mauve. It fastens with a zip down the front, concealed by gilt teat studs.

ROYAL SCOTS DRAGOON GUARDS

Fig.1d

Fig.1a

Fig.1b

Fig.1c

Fig.2d

Fig.2a

Fig.2b

Fig.2c

No.13 Dress – Temperate Barrack Dress
Fig.4a Colonel (late RSDG) in an issue 'woolly pully'. **Fig.4b** The original green shoulder straps have been removed and replaced by these khaki barathea shoulder straps. These have been fitted with gold anodised rank badges and the shoulder strap fastens with a brown leather button. **Fig.4b** He has retained his grey RSDG beret, which is now worn with his staff badge. It is a common practice for staff officers to retain their original berets. **Fig.4d** Shows the red gorget patches worn by on his shirt. These are fastened to the collar by small metal clips on the back. A medium size of these are worn on Service Dress and a larger version on No.1 Dress, both of which are permanently attached to the uniform.

Fig.5 Anodised cap badge. This combined the 'eagle' badge of the Royal Scots Greys with the 'rifles' of the 3rd Carabiniers. **Fig.6a** Anodised collar badge and **Fig.6b** Wire embroidered collar badge, worn no No.1 Dress and Mess Dress.

In 1922 the 3rd Dragoon Guards amalgamated with the 6th Dragoon Guards to form the 3rd Carabiniers. The new badge combined the Prince of Wales's feathers of the 3rd DG, with the crossed rifles of the 6th DG. When the RSDG were formed in 1971, the crossed rifles were incorporated in the new cap badge. This left the PoW plumes, which were adopted as a regimental arm badge, worn on the upper left arm by all ranks. **Fig.7a** Wire embroidered version, on a yellow backing, for Officers' No.1 Dress. **Fig.7b** Wire embroidered version on a blue background, for Officers in No.2 Dress and Other Ranks in No.1 Dress. **Fig.7c** Embroidered version, worn by Other Ranks on No.2 Dress.

Fig.8a Ordnance issue, dark blue beret, as originally approved for the RSDG. This was adopted on the formation of the RSDG. The cap badge was worn with a black backing. However, it was not long until the regiment adopted the distinctive grey beret, previously worn by 'The Greys'. Similar to 'Greys' this was purchased from the PRI shop, Other Ranks wore it as a dress item, but not in the Tank Park, or on exercise, where it might be soiled. Officers also wore it - including the Tank Park and on exercise! **Fig.8b** Ordnance issue grey beret, with cap badge and black backing. Official approval was eventually given for this and, in the early 1980s, it became an issue item. The first mention of it appears in the 1982 issue of Section CF, Headdress and Accessories (Men). Thereafter, dark blue berets were no longer worn by the regiment.

Fig.9 Stable belt

Fig.10a NCOs' arm badge, worn by Corporals and above, on No.2 Dress. **Fig.10b** Embroidered NCOs' arm badge, for wear on No.1 Dress and Mess Dress. **Fig.11** Commanding Officers' tank and Land Rover crew's arm badge. **Fig.12** Regimental Tactical Recognition Flash, introduced in 2004. **Fig.13** Sergeants' chevrons for No.1 Dress, of gold thistle lace on yellow.

Fig.14 Rank slides. These come in a variety of colours and shades, bronze on DPM and black on DPM. Black on green, corporals' rank slide shown here. Bronze on Desert DPM, Lt-Colonel illustrated right.

Fig.3a

Fig.3b

Fig.3c

Fig.4d

Fig.4a

Fig.4b

Fig.4d

Fig.6a

Fig.5

Fig.6b

Fig.7a

Fig.7b

Fig.7c

Fig.8a

Fig.8b

Fig.9

Fig.10a

Fig.10b

Fig.11

Fig.12

Fig.13

Fig.14

ROYAL SCOTS GREYS

No.1 Dress

Forage Cap – All Ranks, blue, with a white vandyke band and a white welt around the crown. This was worn with a metal cap badge, on a black felt backing.
Jacket – All Ranks, blue, with shoulder chains, Other Ranks had the standard collar badges, while Officers wore wire embroidered thistles on their collars. Chevrons consisted of gold thistle lace, on a blue backing. WOs' badges were also gold embroidered on blue. The NCOs arm badge was embroidered in silver on blue.
Trousers – All Ranks, blue, with a single yellow stripe, 1¾ inches wide.

Fig.1a Cap badge, this was worn with a black backing. The black backings, worn behind most of their badges, was in commemoration of their Colonel-in-Chief, the late Tsar Nicolas II, who was murdered by the Bolsheviks in 1918. **Fig.1b** Officers' collar badge for No.1 Dress. A bronze version was worn on Service Dress. All collar badges were worn with black backings. **Fig.1c** Other Ranks' silver anodised collar badge, as worn on No.2 Dress. **Fig.1d** Special pattern of cap badge, used only by the regimental bandsmen.

Fig.2a Silver NCOs' arm badge, used by NCOs and WOs on battledress and No.2 Dress. This badge was on a black backing, which was cut to the shape of the badge. **Fig.2b** Embroidered NCOs' arm badge, worn on No.1 Dress and Mess Dress. **Fig.3** Gilding metal shoulder title, for Other Ranks on battledress. A gold anodised version of this was later worn on No.2 Dress.

No.6 Dress – Tropical Dress.

In 1962, the regiment moved to Aden, with 'C' Squadron attached to the 48th Gurkha Infantry Brigade, in Hong Kong. The regiment remained in these locations until 1964, when it returned to Fallingbostel in Germany. **Fig.4a** Corporal in standard 1950 Pattern issue Jungle Green uniform. This consisted of an aertex jacket, which could be worn with either Green Drill shorts, or trousers, both of which were fastened at the waist with cross-over straps attached to buckles at the side of the garment. He is wearing a grey beret, complete with cap badge and black backing. **Fig.4b** In warm weather the jacket could be worn as a shirt, tucked into the shorts, or trousers This was usually worn with the issue Pattern 1944 web belt. He is also wearing the matching Green Drill bush hat. **Fig.4c** Printed formation sign, worn by the 48th Gurkha Infantry Brigade.

No.10 Dress – Temperate Mess Dress

Other Ranks – 1939 Pattern jacket of scarlet cloth, with a dark blue roll collar and pointed cuffs. No buttons, or shoulder straps, but badges and chevrons as for No.1 Dress. A navy blue, silk cummerbund, five inches wide, completed the uniform.

Other Items of Dress

Beret – The Ordnance issue beret, for The Greys, was the standard dark blue beret. This was worn with the metal cap badge on a black backing. In the late 1940s and early 1950s, various badges and embellishments were adopted, to display regimental pride and tradition, in this drab uniform. During this period The Greys adopted their distinctive grey beret, which was not an issue item, but was purchased from the PRI shop. Other Ranks wore it as a dress item, though not in the Tank Park, nor on exercise, where it might be soiled. Officers also wore it, including in the Tank Park and on exercise.

ROYAL SCOTS GREYS

Fig.1a

Fig.1b

Fig.1c

Fig.2a

Fig.2b

Fig.1d

Fig.3

Fig.4a

Fig.4c

Fig.4b

ROYAL TANK REGIMENT

No.1 Dress

Beret – the Royal Tank Regiment wear a black version, which special distinction can be traced back to the formation of the Royal Tank Corps in 1923.

Jacket – All Ranks, blue.. Other Ranks wear the standard issue collar badges, while Officers wear a slightly larger, silver and gilt version. Chevrons and WOs' badges are embroidered gold on black. All Ranks wear the regimental 'Tank' arm badge on the right upper-arm. ORs have fixed shoulder straps, of the same blue material as the jacket, while Officers have detachable shoulder straps. Officers use the standard pattern of rank badges, with enamel.

Trousers – All Ranks, blue, with a single black mohair band, 2-inches wide.

Fig.1a 2/Lt S Montague-Jones, in No.1 Dress, Non-Ceremonial. This uniform was originally made in 1957, by Conway Williams, London & Camberley, probably for a National Service Officer. It was bought, or acquired, by Montague-Jones in about 1959, when he commenced his own National Service. **Fig.1b** Plain blue collar, with silver and gilt collar badge. **Fig.1c** Silver embroidered tank arm badge, worn on the right arm. **Fig.1d** Plain blue, detachable shoulder strap, held in place with a screw-post type button. **Fig.1e** Pointed cuff, with two buttons and also the black mohair band worn on his trousers.

Fig.2a Capt. RF Constant, in No.1 Dress, ceremonial and wearing white leather gloves. **Fig.2b** This uniform was originally made in 1961, by Conway Williams, identical to that in Fig.1. However, in about 1969, the RTR introduced a modified pattern of jacket, with a black mohair braided collar. This jacket has thus been modified to the new standard pattern. **Fig.2c** Above the left breast pocket are the Army Flying wings and ribbon for UN Cyprus medal. **Fig.2d** Side fastening of the gold and black waist sash, worn only by officers of the RTR, in this order of dress. His sword belt is worn under the jacket, with only the gold on blue sword slings showing. The sword is carried in its dress, plated scabbard and is fitted with a gold sword knot. **Fig.2e** Detachable, gold cord shoulder strap, for ceremonial dress.

No.2 Dress

Fig.3a 1st RTR Lcpl, in 1980 Pattern No.2 Dress uniform, as identified by the plain patch breast pockets. **Fig.3b** Insignia on the right arm, consisting of the single rank chevron, regimental 'tank' arm badge and crossed swords. The latter badge indicates that he is an Assistant Physical Training Instructor. **Fig.3c** Insignia on the left arm, in addition to the rank chevron, a red lanyard, worn only by 1 RTR. **Fig.3d** Other Ranks' dress belt. A black leather belt, with similar buckle, was introduced in 1953 for wear with No.1 Dress. This was replaced, in the early 1960s, by this black plastic belt, which was also worn with No.2 Dress.

Up until 1960, all regiments of the Royal Tank Regiment wore a black cord lanyard, with the exception of 1st RTR who wore a red cord lanyard. With the adoption on No.2 Dress, for ORs, in the early 1960s, the wearing of shoulder strap flashes was ceased. Thus to distinguish the individual RTR regiments, lanyards in the regimental colours were introduced. **Fig.4a** Red cord lanyard for 1st RTR **Fig.4b** Black cord lanyard, worn by all other RTR regiments, until the early 1960s. **Fig.4c** Saffron lanyard, 2nd RTR. **Fig.4d** Green cord lanyard, 3rd RTR. **Fig.4e** Blue cord lanyard, 4th RTR. This was later replaced by a blue lanyard, similar in construction to the saffron one worn by 2nd RTR. **Fig.4f** Red and light blue lanyard, 5th RTR.

ROYAL TANK REGIMENT

Fig.1a

Fig.1b

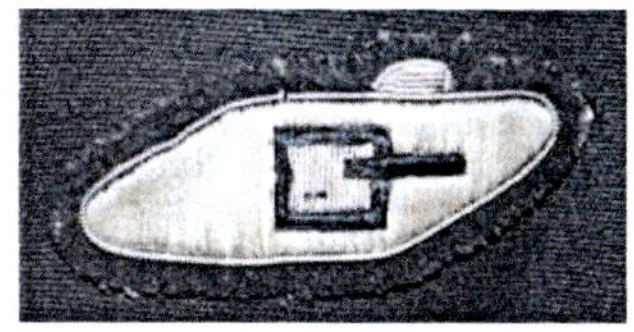
Fig.1c

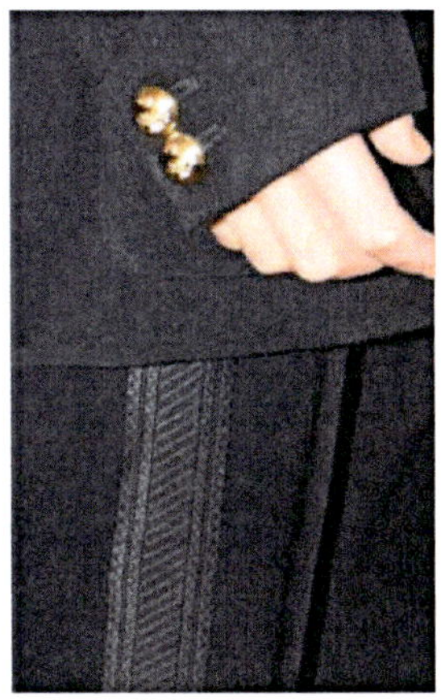
Fig.1e

Fig.1d

Fig.2a

Fig.2b

Fig.2c

Fig.2d

Fig.2e

Fig.3a

Fig.3d

Fig.3b

Fig.3c

Fig.4a

Fig.4b

Fig.4c

Fig.4d

Fig.4e

Fig.4f

Fig.5a

Fig.5b

Fig.5c

Fig.6a

Fig.6b

Fig.6c

Fig.6d

Fig.6e

Fig.6f

Fig.7a

Fig.7b

Fig.5a Cap badge. Early cap badges had Tudor (King's) crowns and were made in white metal for Other Ranks and silver for officers. In the mid-1950s, a new pattern with St Edward's (Queen's) crown began to be issued. Other Ranks' badges were made in silver anodised, as here, while officers bought silver, or silver plated badges. In the 1990s All ranks began to be issued with a cap badge in bright silver. While serving in Northern Ireland, it became common practice for soldiers to paint their cap badges black, to make them less conspicuous. Later, a black version could be obtained from the PRI shop. **Fig.5b** Other Ranks' woven beret badge, with merrow edge. These also became popular in the army, being adopted and worn by some regiments for tactical purposes. **Fig.5c** Officers' wire embroidered cap badge, worn on the officers' Astrakhan dress beret. For a short time in the 1970s, it was also worn by officers of 2nd RTR, on their normal black berets. Early examples of this badge have been noted incorrectly manufactured with a Tudor (King's) crown.

Fig.6a Other Ranks' white metal collar badge, with Tudor (King's) crown. This was manufactured in this size and in a slightly larger version. These were worn on No.1 Dress and by some regiments on battledress. **Fig.6b** Officers' bronze collar badge, for Service Dress and Battledress. Slight variations exist in size and colour. **Fig.6c** Officers' silver and gilt collar badges, used on No.1 and No.3 Dress. The new patterns of collar badges, with St. Edwards (Queen's) crowns, were slightly larger than the previous patterns. **Fig.6d** ORs' silver anodised collar badge. **Fig.6e** Officers' bronze collar badge. **Fig.6f** Officers' silver and gilt collar badge.

With the introduction of No.2 Dress for Other Ranks, in 1962, new patterns of ceremonial berets were introduced for both ORs and Officers. **Fig.7a** Other Ranks' ceremonial beret, with a 1-inch wide leather headband and a large internal backing piece, which gave the beret this "*set up*" for the badge and hackle. The ORs' hackle was a wedge shape, constructed from green, red and brown feathers. **Fig.7b** Officers' ceremonial beret, made from imitation black Astrakhan, with a black braid band and two rows of gold braid. A wire embroidered badge and an officers' pattern hackle was worn on it. The green, red and brown hackle was much more three-dimensional than the pattern worn by ORs. These were not popular items of headwear and were abandoned in the late 1970s.

Fig.8a Captain, in the 1950s, wearing Service Dress. This particular jacket had been made in 1941, but continued in use after the war. He has a black beret, black cord lanyard and brown Sam Browne belt. The latter was worn by all RTR Officers until 1954. **Fig.8b** Gold anodised RTR button with Tudor (King's) crown. Anodised buttons were introduced in the early 1950s, before the introduction of the St Edward's (Queen's) crown pattern. **Fig.8c** Insignia worn on the right arm. In addition to the regimental 'tank' arm badge, the formation sign of Lancashire ACF (Army Cadet Force). **Fig.8d** Insignia on the left arm.

Fig.9a 2/Lt S Montague-Jones, 8th RTR, a National Service officer, see Figs.1 and 9 for his other uniforms. He is wearing the standard pattern of Service Dress, with the black Sam Browne belt, introduced in 1954. On closer examination, there is evidence of it having previously been worn by a Captain, and there are still cut threads on the inside, which had once secured the medal ribbons. For those serving a short period, it is not unusual to acquire used uniforms, as opposed to spending large sums of money on new items. **Fig.9b** Officers' regimental pattern lanyard, of three thin black cords entwined together to make a thick cord. Other Ranks in this regiment wore the standard pattern. See Fig.4b. **Fig.9c** Right arm showing tank badge and pointed cuff without buttons. **Fig.9d** Box pleated breast pocket, with three-point flap.

Fig.8a

Fig.8b

Fig.8c

Fig.8d

Fig.9a

Fig.9b

Fig.9c

Fig.9d

Fig.10a Major AG Whitfield, 4th RTR, 1976, in the new, cavalry pattern of Service Dress in Ceremonial Order. In about 1969, an attempt was made to standardise the pattern of Service Dress worn by the whole of the Royal Armoured Corps, including the Royal Tank Regiment. It was to follow the cavalry pattern, made from khaki whipcord material, with plain breast pockets, jetted side pockets and plain cuffs with a vent, which were closed with two buttons. Officers already serving would wear out their regimental pattern of Service Dress. He has his dress beret and full size Campaign Service Medal, with the bar for Northern Ireland. He is equipped with a black Sam Browne and frog, with a black sword knot on the standard Infantry pattern sword. **Fig.10b** Shows the right arm, with tank badge and plain cuff, the vent closed by two buttons. **Fig.10c** Left breast pocket, without a centre pleat. The oblong flap is 2½ inches deep and has rounded corners.

No.3 Dress – Tropical Ceremonial Uniform

Fig.11a Captain wearing No.3 Dress. This is the tropical version of No.1 Dress, made in white drill material, for ceremonial wear in warm climates. This uniform was worn in the late 1950s. Despite the black Sam Browne, introduced in 1954, the original Tudor (King's) crown buttons and badges have been retained. The buttons are attached to the uniform with split rings, ie "Bachelor buttons", which enabled them to be easily removed for the cleaning of the uniform. Officers, who had previously worn brown Sam Browne belts, had them polished black to conform to the new pattern. However, they still retained their original insignia. **Fig.11b** Right arm showing wire embroidered 'tank' arm badge and pointed cuff with two vent buttons. **Fig.11c** Detachable shoulder strap. For ceremonial duties wire cord shoulder straps could be fitted, see Fig.2e.

No.5 Dress – Battledress

Like the rest of the Army, a variety of issue battledress uniforms were worn, with a few officers obtaining superior quality items from their tailors. After 1945 there were eight separate RTR regiments in existence and, just like the cavalry regiments, they also took pride in their unit and had their own regimental embellishments.

Fig.12a Trooper, 3rd RTR, in 1949 Pattern battledress, with khaki Pattern 1937 web belt. **Fig.12b** Battledress showing insignia. In addition to the regimental 'tank' arm badge, black cord lanyard and formation signs, he has the green tape bands of 3rd RTR on his shoulder straps. **Fig.12c** Embroidered 11th Armoured Division formation sign, worn in pairs, with the black bull facing the front.

Unlike No.2 dress above, the eight regiments had the following special embellishments: 1st RTR wore a red lanyard, see Fig.4a, while the rest had black cord lanyards. Coloured flashes were worn on the shoulder straps of the seven remaining regiments. These were made from braid, felt, or ribbon, or whatever materials could be procured locally. Thus variations in materials and colours exist for most regiments. **Fig.13a** 2nd RTR used a yellow flash, with the RTR colours in the centre (green, red and brown) and the green facing the wearer's front. 3rd RTR had a green flash, see Figs.12 and 24. **Fig.13b** 4th RTR blue flash, **Fig.13c** 5th RTR red over light blue flash. **Fig.13d** 6th RTR red over yellow. **Fig.13e** 7th RTR red over green. 8th RTR red over dark blue, see Fig.14. These flashes were originally worn on battledress, but with the introduction of No.2 Dress in 1962, they moved to the pullover and black coveralls.

Fig.10a

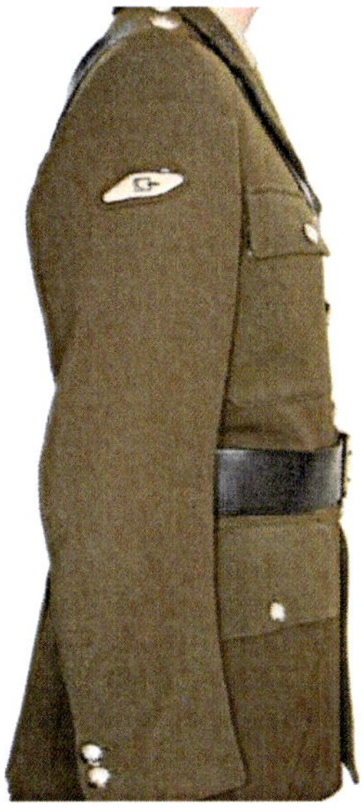

Fig.10b

Fig.10c

Fig.11a

Fig.11b

Fig.11c

Fig.12c

Fig.12a

Fig.12b

Fig.13a

Fig.13b

Fig.13c

Fig.13d

Fig.13e

Fig.14c

Fig.14d

Fig.14a

Fig.14b

Fig.15c

Fig.15a

Fig.15b

Fig.14a 2/Lt S Montague-Jones, 8th RTR, a National Service officer, see Figs.1 and 9 for his other uniforms. He is wearing the issue 1949 Pattern Battledress, with black beret and a black Pattern 1937 web belt. In 1954, the RTR were authorised to blacken their khaki webbing. Oil and grease, from working on armoured vehicles, were difficult to remove from their khaki web belts. This, together with the adoption of black Sam Browne belts at the same time, therefore made sense. In addition to the bronze St Edward's (Queen's) crown collar badges, black leather "football" type buttons have been added to the exposed buttons, on both his blouse and trousers. This was a common practice for all RTR Officers on their battledress. He is also wearing his regimental Officers' pattern of black lanyard, see Fig.9b. **Fig.14b** Shows the distribution of embellishments worn on his blouse. Initially, RTR officers were to follow the practice of the RAC, wearing rank badges embroidered on a yellow backing. The colonel of 3rd RTR thought that these would clash with their green flash, so they adopted embroidered rank badges on a khaki backing. During the 1950s, the RTR officers' rank insignia was in a period of fluidity. In about 1953, officers in the 8th RTR changed from yellow backed embroidered rank insignia to metal insignia. By the late 1950s the 1st, 6th, 7th, and 8th RTR were wearing metal rank badges, the 2nd, 4th and 5th RTR were wearing embroidered rank badges, on yellow backings. **Fig.14c** Embroidered 7th Armoured Brigade formation sign, worn in pairs with the jerboa 'rat' facing the front. **Fig.14d** 8th RTR flash, red over dark blue, with metal rank star.

Fig.15a 2/Lt, Territorial Officer in 1949 Pattern Battledress. **Fig.15b** Battledress blouse, showing distribution of badges and embellishments. The blouse has bronze St Edward's (Queen's) crown collar badges, black cord lanyard, black leather "football" type buttons, gilt and enamel rank stars, 'tank' arm badge and also formation signs. **Fig.15c** Embroidered sign worn by 22nd Armoured Brigade (TA), who were part of 56th (London) Armoured Division (TA). These were worn in pairs, with the stags head facing the front.

On the right arm, All Ranks of the Royal Tank Regiment, wear a special regimental arm badge, which depicts the "rhomboidal" tank used during The Great War. Designed by Colonel (later Major-General) Ernest Swinton, in 1917, this continues in wear to the present day. Even since 1946, numerous variations in manufacture have existed.' These include details of the sponson, together the 6 Pounder gun, which is either level, or inclined at 15 degrees. **Fig.16a** Tank arm badge, embroidered in white on khaki, outlined in black thread. Some officers wore a padded version of this. **Fig.16b** Other Ranks' tank arm badge. Although manufactured on a rectangular backing, they were normally cut to shape before being applied to the uniform. **Fig.16c** Tank arm badge, in silver wire on black, for No.1 and No.3 Dress. **Fig.16d** Tank arm badge, in gold wire on black, used by the band. **Fig.16e** Gilding metal arm badge, with black felt backing, worn on tropical uniforms. An anodised version of this also exists.

Fig.17a Gilding metal shoulder title, worn by Other Ranks on their greatcoats. **Fig.17b** Small gilding metal shoulder title, designed for tropical uniforms. The wearing of regimental coloured arm flashes on the shoulder straps of most uniforms, meant that the metal titles were seldom worn.

Fig.18a Colonel serving in the Far East, in a locally tailored version of No.6 Dress. He has the Staff badge on his black beret and red gorget patches on his collar. **Fig.18b** Right arm, showing 'tank' arm badge. **Fig.18c** Shoulder strap, showing anodised rank badges.

Fig.16a

Fig.16b

Fig.16c

Fig.16d

Fig.16e

Fig.17a

Fig.17b

Fig.18a

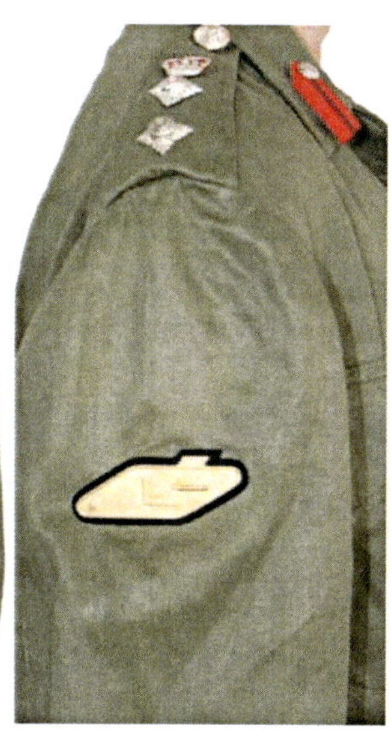

Fig.18b

Fig.18c

No.6 Dress – Warm weather parade uniform (Bush Jacket).
Fig.19a Staff Sergeant D Dawson BEM, 1st RTR, wearing the early pattern of No.6 Dress. This is made from stone-coloured twill cloth, in a combination of polyester and cotton. In the 1980s, consequent on the introduction on a new pattern of No.2 Dress, with plain patch breast pockets, a new pattern of No.6 Dress, with similar breast pockets, was introduced. This new pattern was made from a slightly different material, hence there is a slight colour difference. The red cord lanyard, on the left arm, indicates 1st RTR, hence there was no need for the coloured shoulder strap flashes. **Fig.19b** Insignia worn on the right arm, with the 'tank' arm badge worn between the chevrons and crown. He has the standard No.2 Dress rank insignia, of a new pattern introduced for this order of dress. These are embroidered on a backing that matches this uniform. However, a tropical version of the 'tank' arm badge has not been introduced. **Fig.19c** Medal ribbons for the British Empire Medal, 1939/45 Star, France and Germany Star, Defence Medal, War Medal 1939-45 and the Army Long Service and Good Conduct Medal. **Fig.19d** No.6 Dress trousers. These are made from a similar material to the jacket, with side pockets. There are also two hip pockets and adjustment buckles are fitted at either side.

No.7 Dress – Warm weather barrack dress.
Fig.20a Trooper, 1st RTR in No.7 Dress. Like the S/Sgt above, the regiment is identified by the red lanyard. The short sleeved, stone coloured shirt is made from polyester and cotton and is fitted with breast pockets and shoulder straps. **Fig.20b** No.7 Dress stone coloured trousers, made from polyester and viscose. These are similar to No.6 trousers regarding the pockets, but thin, narrow belt loops are fitted. These can be compared with Fig.19d, opposite.

No.10 Dress – Temperate Mess Dress
Fig.21a Sergeant wearing Temperate Mess Dress. The 1939 pattern jacket is of dark blue barathea, with a roll collar faced with black cloth. It has three small regimental buttons down the front of each side and a further two buttons on each cuff. He is wearing issue collar badges and miniature medal for the Campaign Service Medal, with the Northern Ireland bar. **Fig.21b** Right arm showing the gold on black rank chevrons. Though these are $^{2}/_{3}$rd size, the regulations state that the 'tank' arm badge is not, however, it is not uncommon to see it being worn. **Fig.21c** Twisted cord shoulder strap and button. **Fig.21d** Scarlet Mess Vest, this has a U-front and is fitted with four small regimental buttons.

No.14 Dress – Shirt Sleeve Order
Fig.22a 2nd RTR wearing the Other Ranks' issue khaki shirt and green barrack dress trousers. These trousers were issued for wear with summer, or winter Barrack Dress, thus avoiding undue wear on the No.2 Dress trousers. **Fig.22b** Rank slide for both 1st and 2nd RTR, post 1992, with the brown worn to the front. **Fig.23** Stable belt.

Fig.24a Captain, 3rd RTR, wearing the Officers pattern fawn shirt and Service Dress trousers. **Fig.24b** Left arm with rank slide. **Fig.24c** 3rd RTR, troopers' rank slide.

Fig.25 Corporals' brassard/pen holder, worn on the black coveralls. **Fig.26** 2nd RTR troopers' rank slide. **Fig.27** Rank slide worn by bandsmen and extra regimentally employed (ERE) personnel. **Fig.28** 1st/2nd RTR sergeants' rank slide. **Fig.29** RTR instructors' rank slide. These rank slides were generally worn on shirts, pullovers and coveralls.

Fig.19b

Fig.19a

Fig.19c

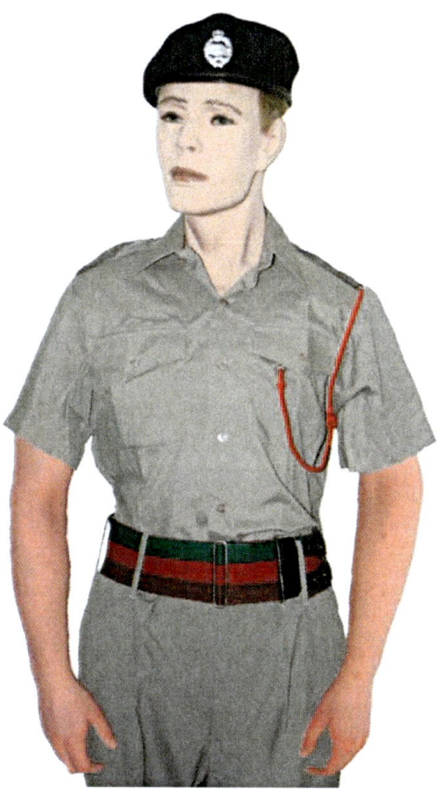

Fig.20a

Fig.20b

Fig.19d

Fig.21a

Fig.21c

Fig.21b

Fig.21d

Fig.22a

Fig.22b

Fig.23

Fig.24a

Fig.24b

Fig.24c

Fig.26

Fig.27

Fig.25

Fig.28

Fig.29

TANK SUITS AND COVERALLS

During the latter part of the Second World War, three different types of tank suits had been developed. These patterns continued in use for about twenty years after the war.

Fig.1a The first of these is the 'pixie suit', or more properly the Temperate Tank Oversuit. This was introduced in July 1943 and was still listed in the Clothing Catalogues in the early-1980s. The oversuit was made from a heavy weight cotton, in light khaki and was lined throughout with khaki angola, shirt type, material. It was a well-designed garment, with reinforced knees, elbows, and seat, with thirteen pockets and a detachable hood. Designed to be worn over battledress, it was fitted with two full length zip fasteners. The shoulder straps were also specially strengthened, allowing them to be used when pulling casualties from the vehicle. In 1954, for administrative purposes, the tank suit and hood were accounted for separately, each with its new stores code number.

Fig.1b Helmet, Royal Armoured Corps, Mk.2. Both the Mark 1 and Mark 2 RAC steel helmets had been developed during the war and, while their bodies were similar in shape, their liners were different. The Mk.1 helmet liner was fixed in position with a nut and bolt through the top of the helmet. The Mk.2 helmet liner was held in place with a Lift-The-Dot fastener, fastened to a spigot, riveted to the inside top of the helmet. The Mk.1 helmet was still being listed in the Clothing Catalogues until 1960, while the Mk.2 helmet was still listed in the 1976 catalogue. Both helmets could be fitted with either a plain elasticated chin strap or, as shown here, the RAC quick release chin strap.

Fig.1c Only a skeleton version of Pattern 1937 web equipment was worn by crewmen. In addition to the web belt, pistol case and pistol ammunition pouch, braces and brace attachments could also be worn. The RAC, pistol case, Mk.2, shown here, was introduced during the war and could be worn either on, or below, the waist belt. This was later replaced with the Pattern 1958 web equipment. The Enfield No.2 Mk. I*, .380 revolver, shown here, was introduced in 1938. This was a variant of the standard revolver, without the spur on the hammer, which it was felt could catch on clothing, or equipment, especially in confined spaces. Unfortunately, this meant that it could only be fired double-action, making accuracy more difficult. A khaki cord lanyard was attached to the revolver ring, the other end being worn round either the wearer's neck, arm, or around his waist belt.

The second 'tank suit', introduced in September 1944, was the Denim Tank Overall, in khaki- green, which fastened down the front with a series of removable buttons. Like the tank oversuit, it was fitted with internal braces for casualty evacuation and a large number of pockets. The left breast pocket was noticeable in being fitted with two rows of pencil pockets. This item continued in wear until the late 1960s.

The third 'tank suit', introduced at about the same time as the Denim Tank Overall, was the Tropical Tank Suit, in green, mosquito-proof cotton fabric, similar in design to the Denim Tank Overall.

Fig.1a

Fig.1b

Fig.1c

Fig.2 1953 Pattern, tank suit, which was almost identical to the previous pattern. The only difference being the shoulder straps, which are the full width of the garment, with the overlap being sewn on the inside of the garment. The Tropical Tank Suit is shown here with the green tropical hat.

These were later superseded by a 1968 Pattern, also made from cotton and gabardine.

Fig.3 Pattern 1944 web belt, pistol holster, and pistol ammunition pouch, together with a Enfield No.2 Mk. I*, .380 revolver. This pattern of equipment was restricted to the Far East, where its colour would blend in to the local vegetation. It was also generally used by the airborne forces, being lighter than the normal Pattern 1937 Web Equipment.

In the early-1960s, coveralls began to replace denims as a form of workwear. These were made from a green drill material and fastened with removable buttons, with a black version being issued to the RTR. By the early 1970s, an improved version, made in cloth twill, polyester and cotton material, had been introduced. This had a single breast pocket and the front, shoulder straps and cuffs were now all fastened with popper studs. Again both green and black versions were issued. In the early 1980s, improved versions of both of these, were introduced. The only difference was a slight, unnoticeable difference in the material.

Fig.4 Olive drab Coveralls, polyester and cotton, a pattern listed in the 1982 Clothing Catalogue. **Fig.5** black version, worn by the RTR and normally worn with a black Pattern 1937 web belt, a black on white name tag and a black brassard/pen holder.

Fig.6 By the 1970s, tank suits had become 'Combat Vehicle Crewmen's Coveralls'. A new olive drab, water repellent, Combat Vehicle Crewmen's Coverall, was adopted in the late 1970s. These were similar to ordinary coveralls, but had a permanently fitted hood. Although water repellent, they did have a number of disadvantages. If the wearer became hot, the perspiration was unable to escape, thus making the wearer wet on the inside. The nylon material used would rustle when the wearer moved. Finally, if exposed to heat, like vehicle exhausts, they melted.

Fig.7 In the late 1960s a new helmet had been developed to replace the wartime RAC steel helmet. Made from fibre glass, it had built in headphones, thus giving it a very distinctive shape. It was also fitted with a microphone and wires to enable it to be connected directly into the tank's communications system. While giving good head protection in the moving vehicle, the headphones had to be worn at all times. This meant that it was impossible to hear what was going on nearby. If a headphone was moved from the ear, to hear what was going on, the loose headphone could be heard by anyone in the close vicinity! A special carrying bag was issued, to avoid damage to the helmet.

Suit Tank Tropical
1953 Pattern
SIZE 3
Height 5ft.7—5ft.8
Breast 36—38
Waist 32—34
Leg Seam 31½
Cookson & Clegg Ltd
1956

Fig.3

Fig.4

MACDONALD

Fig.5

COVERALL MEN'S
Green Army Pattern
8405-99-977-3586
SIZE 180/100
Harvey & Co. (Clothing) Ltd.
SL31b/2588

COVERALLS, MENS' BLACK,
ARMY PATTERN
CH 8405-99-977-3594
SIZE 170/100
Bathgate Protective Clothing Ltd
SL31b/2933

Fig.6

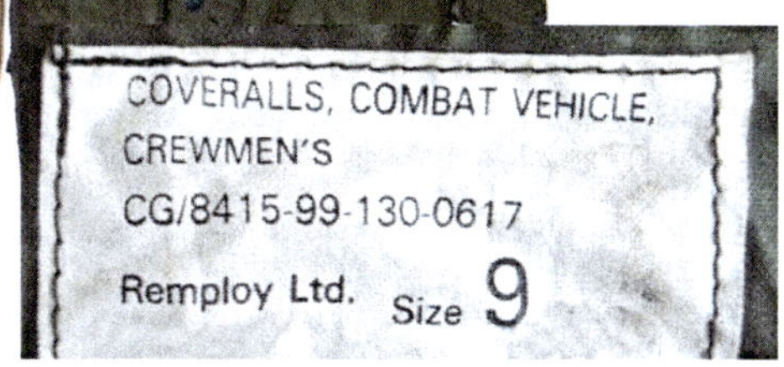
COVERALLS, COMBAT VEHICLE,
CREWMEN'S
CG/8415-99-130-0617
Remploy Ltd. Size 9

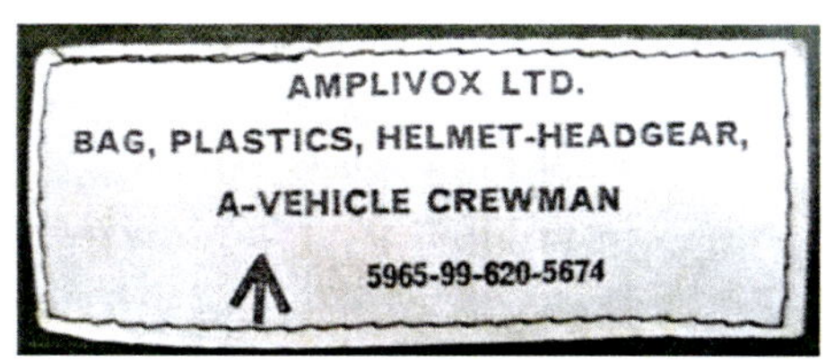
AMPLIVOX LTD.
BAG, PLASTICS, HELMET-HEADGEAR,
A-VEHICLE CREWMAN
5965-99-620-5674

Fig.7

Fig.8 In the 1980s, trials were undertaken on a pattern of coveralls to be worn by Armoured Fighting Vehicle crewmen, in the Arctic. These were made in the standard temperate DPM (Disruptive Pattern Material). The front fastened with a zip, while the pockets and cuffs fastened with Velcro (hook and loop tape). It had a permanently attached hood, with a wired rim. As they have not been noted in the Stores Catalogues, it must be assumed that they were not adopted.

Fig.9 These coveralls would have been worn with the Cold Weather (Arctic) Cap. This was also made in temperate DPM, with a large peak, which could be worn in either the up, or down, position. It was also fitted with ear flaps, which extended around the back of the head. These had an inner green pile lining and, like the peak, these could also be worn either up, or down. This hat was part of the standard cold weather clothing and as such was a normal issue item.

Fig.10 By the mid-1980s, a new pattern of coveralls had been introduced. These were made from a green twill *Aramid* material and were flame resistant. They were similar to the Arctic trials coveralls, with two breast pockets and a clear, map pocket on the right leg. The use of these was restricted to the crewmen of Main Battle Tanks only, and then only for operational use. The first use of these was in the Gulf War of 1990-91.

Fig.11 By this time a new Armoured Vehicle crewman's helmet had been introduced. It consisted of a green fibreglass scalp protector, with cut-outs for the headset, giving the wearer protection to the head, while inside a moving vehicle. A separate set of headphones and microphone, connected to a head harness, was also worn. This is a much more flexible design than the previous pattern and is still being worn.

Fig.12 The Gulf War also saw the first major use of the new 1990 PLCE (Personal Load Carrying Equipment). The actual nomenclature for this is the 1989 version. In addition to the standard equipment, in the main designed for infantry use, a holster was also included. This consisted of five separate components and enabled it to be worn in a number of configurations, either on the belt, or as a shoulder holster. Some of these holsters, for the 9mm Browning pistol, were worn during the Gulf War.

In the early 1990s an improved version of coveralls for combat vehicle crewman were introduced. These were olive drab in colour and were made from fire-retardant Nomex/Kevlar material. However, by the late 1990s, they were no longer listed in the stores catalogue.

Fig.13 By 1996, a special pattern of coveralls, for combat vehicle crewmen, were introduced. These were influenced by the Soldier '95 clothing developments, typified by the rank strap on the front. These coveralls were made from a lightweight twill cottons and synthetic corespun material in temperate DPM, which were also Infra-Red Reflective. As they are not fire-resistant, or fire-retardant, they are only worn on exercise. They are clearly stamped THIS GARMENT IS FOR TRAINING ONLY, to prevent any misuse. They are clearly designed to avoid using the more expensive fire-resistant/retardant clothing while training.

Fig.8

Fig.9

Fig.10

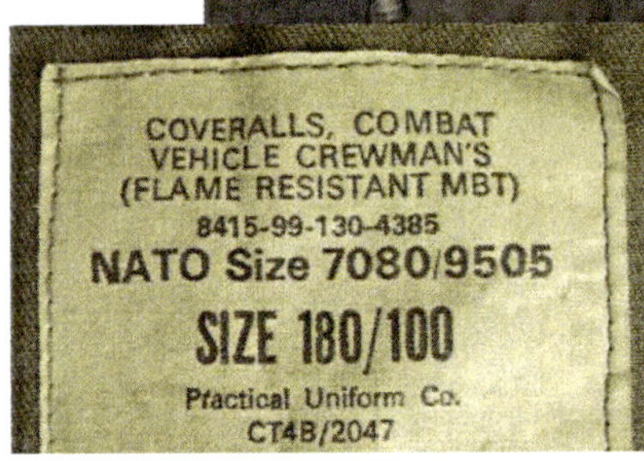

Fig.11

Fig.12

Fig.13

CREWMAN EXERCISE
CG 8415-99-869-2852
HEIGHT / CHEST
SIZE 190/104
CT34b 0954
NAME:
NO:

THIS GARMENT IS
FOR TRAINING ONLY

Fig.14 By the late 1990s, yet another pattern of coveralls were adopted. These were made from an olive, *Aramid*, flame retardant material. They had two breast pockets, two internal breast pockets accessed by zip fasteners, side and leg pockets. The front was fitted with a rank strap and the waist could also be adjusted with an elasticated draw-string. The rear could also be opened for bodily functions, thus avoiding total removal of the coveralls. They were also fitted with an internal harness, to enable easy removal of casualties from the vehicle, see bottom right photo.

Crewmen's helmets are not ballistic and, as such, when operating outside the vehicle a standard Mk.6 combat helmet is worn. The example shown here has been fitted with a temperate DPM cover.

Fig.15 In 2003, armoured troops in the war in Iraq (Operation TELIC) could be seen wearing a beige version of the combat vehicle crewman's coveralls. These fire retardant coveralls are identical to the olive version. A Lieutenant's rank slide, on Desert DPM, is being worn here on the front of the coveralls. He is also wearing a Desert DMP cover on his Mk.6 combat helmet.

Fig.16 At the same time some crewmen were also seen wearing the PLCE Pattern 1990, temperate DPM, shoulder holster. This also came in five separate components and was similar to the olive green version worn previously.

In the late 1990s clothing catalogues for the Army, Navy and Royal Air Force were combined together into tri-service clothing catalogues. This made sense as many items were being used across the services.

Fig.17 In the early 2000's a new pattern of coveralls were introduced. Made in olive, from polyester and cotton, they now had a small slanted breast pocket and also a pocket on the upper left leg. They were fastened down the front, at the cuffs and the ankles with Velcro, hook and loop tape. These were slits at the sides, which enabled access to the side pockets on undergarments. These openings were closed by Velcro. The waist could be adjusted by two tabs at either side, which fastened to strips of Velcro on the back waist of the coveralls. The waist was also fitted with a small extension tab, at the waist front, for ease of opening.

Fig.18 A similar set of coveralls to the above were also manufactures in stone, for wear in the Gulf.

Fig.14

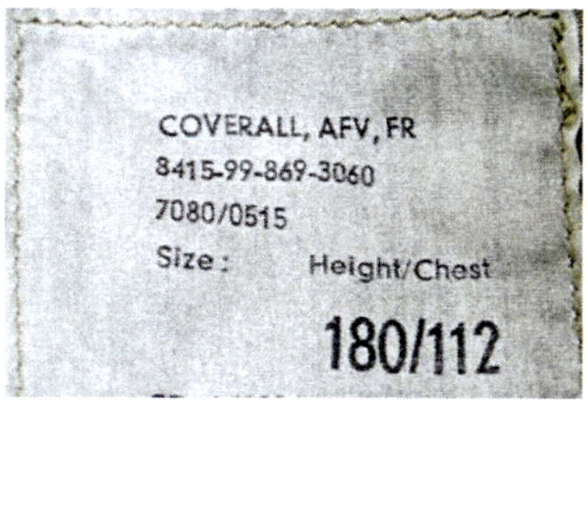
COVERALL, AFV, FR
8415-99-869-3060
7080/0515
Size: Height/Chest
180/112

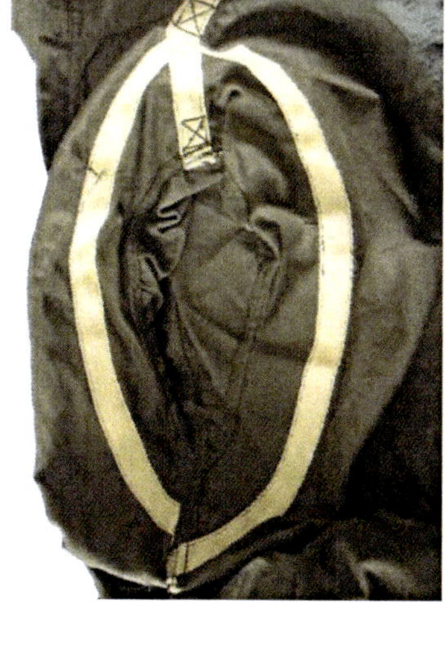

Fig.15

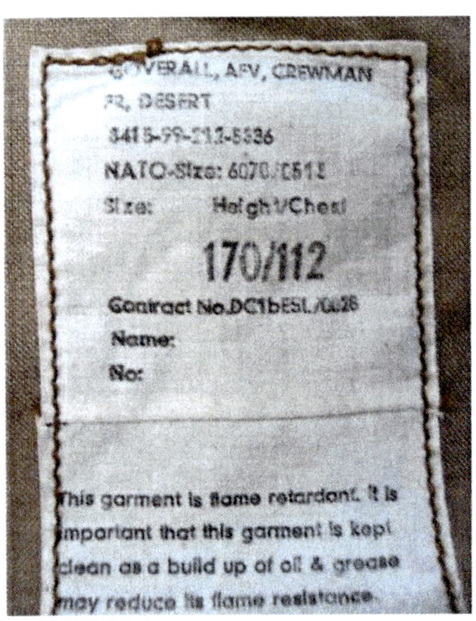
AFV, CREWMAN
DESERT
Size: Height/Chest
170/112
Name:
No:
This garment is flame retardant. It is
important that this garment is kept
clean as a build up of oil & grease
may reduce its flame resistance.

Fig.16

Fig.17

Fig.18

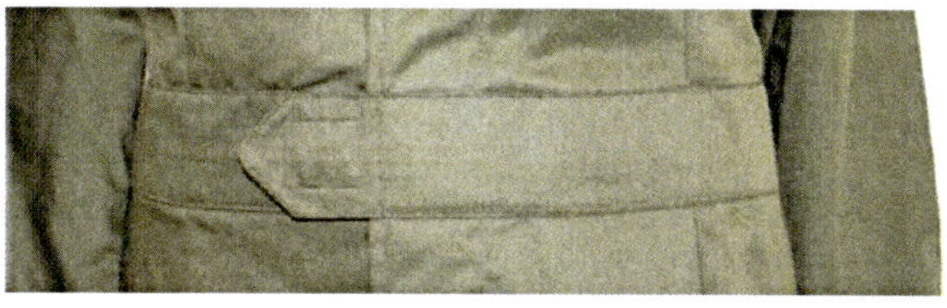

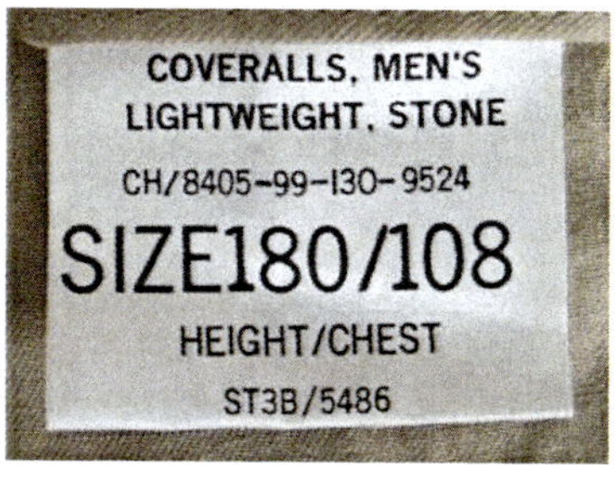
COVERALLS, MEN'S
LIGHTWEIGHT, STONE
CH/8405-99-130-9524
SIZE180/108
HEIGHT/CHEST
ST3B/5486

BIBLIOGRAPHY

Army List
Army Orders
Army Council Instructions
List of Changes

Catalogue of Clothing and Necessaries
Section CB - Armlets, Badges, Chevrons and Titles, 1949, 1959, 1963 and 1973
Section CC – Underclothing, Necessaries and related items, 1958 and 1965
Section CE – Ceremonial Equipment, 1970
Section CF – Headwear and Relative Accessories, 1958, 1965 and 1973
Section CG - Battle and Service Dress, Combat and Physical Training Clothing, Greatcoats 1959 and 1962
Section CH – Tropical, Waterproof, Protective and Anti-Gas Clothing, 1960
Section CH – Hospital, Protective (including industrial) Waterproof, Tropical (other then Ceremonial) and Anti-Gas Clothing, 1966
Section CJ – Anti-Gas Clothing, 1949
Section CL – Officers' Clothing and Necessaries, 1949
Section CM – Cold Climate Clothing, 1949
Section CN – Accoutrements and Steel Helmets, 1960 and 1965
Section CP – No.1 Dress and No.3 Dress, 1959 and 1962

Catalogue of Ordnance Stores and Ammunition
Section CB – Badges of Rank, Service Organization and Qualification, 1978, 1980, 1982, 1984, 1987, 1993, 1995 and 1997
Section CE – Ceremonial Equipment, 1980, 1986, 1993, 1995 and 1997
Section CF – Headdress and Accessories/Headwear, 1979, 1982, 1985, 1991, 1994, 1995 and 1997
Section CG – Combat Dress (Temperate and Tropical) NBC Clothing, 1982, 1986, 1993, 1995 and 1997
Section CH – Hospital, Protective and Barrack Dress, 1977, 1982, 1986, 1992, 1994, 1996 and 1997
Section CM – 1986, 1994 and 1996
Section CN – Accoutrements and Steel Helmets, 1976, 1984, 1985, 1991, 1993, 1995, 1997 and 1999
Section CP – Service Dress (Men) No.1, No.2, No.3 and No.6 Dress, 1977, 1980, 1986, 1993 and 1997

Clothing Regulations
Pamphlet No.3 – Officers' Clothing, 1953 and 1965
Pamphlet No.4 – Scales of Clothing for Men, 1953 and 1964
Pamphlet No.8 – Full Dress, No.1 Dress and No.3 Dress, 1953 (1958), 1962 and 1967
Pamphlet No.10 – Instructions for the Wearing of the Insignia of Orders, Decorations and Medals and Medal Ribbons, 1961
Pamphlet No.15 – Badges, Chevrons, Titles and Embellishments, and Head-Dress, 1966
Pamphlet No.16 – No.10 (Temperate) and No.11 (Tropical) Mess Dress for Warrant Officers and Sergeants and Coloured Side Hats (Army Code No.14991) 1967

Materiel Regulations for the Army, Vol.3 - Clothing
Pamphlet No.3 – Scales for Officers of the Regular Army, 1993 and 1996
Pamphlet No.4 – Scales of Clothing for Soldiers, 1975 and 1993
Pamphlet No.8 – No.1 and No.3 Dress, 1971, 1986 and 1994
Pamphlet No.10 – Instructions for the Wearing of the Insignia of Orders, Decorations and Medals, 1972, 1981 and 1995
Pamphlet No.15 – Badges, Embellishments and Head-Dress, 1980 and 1995
Pamphlet No.16 – Optional Items of Dress, 1982 and 1995

Dress Regulations for the Army, 1934

Rules Relating to Dress
Pamphlet No.1 – Officers, 1955
Pamphlet No.2 – Other Ranks (Male) 1956
Pamphlet No.4 – Officers Ceremonial Dress Table and Guide to the Correct Order of Dress, 1954

Dress Regulations for Officers of the Army
Pamphlet No.1 – General Instructions, 1969, 1983 and 1995
Pamphlet No.3 – Royal Armoured Corps, 1972 and 1995

Regimental Dress Regulations, etc.
Dress Regulations for Officers of the 3rd Carabiniers, August 1958
5th Royal Inniskilling Dragoon Guards, tailor's notes
Royal Scots Greys, tailor's notes on No.1 Dress and Service Dress
Royal Hussars tailor's notes
14th/20th King's Hussars tailor's notes
Officers' Dress Regulations, 15th/19th The Kings Royal Hussars, 1981, also tailor's notes
16th/5th The Queen's Royal Lancers, Officer's Dress Regulations c.1958, 1966, 1988 and tailor's notes
Standing Orders of the 17th/21st Lancers, February 1968 and tailor's notes
Royal Tank Regiment Dress Regulations 1955

Authorised and Registered Army Formation Badges, Defence Publicity (Army) Nov. 2004
Authorised and Registered Tactical Recognition Flashes (TRFs) Defence Publicity (Army) November 2004

Regimental Magazines
The Regimental Journal of 1st The Queen's Dragoon Guards
Eagle and Carbine, Regimental Journal of the Royal Scots Dragoon Guards
4/7th Royal Dragoon Guards Regimental Magazine
5th Royal Inniskilling Dragoon Guards Journal
The Journal of The Queen's Own Hussars
The Crossbelts, The Journal of the Queen's Royal Irish Hussars
The Delhi Spearman, Regimental Journal of the 9th/12th Royal Lancers
The Royal Hussars Journal
The Lilywhites, The Journal of the 13th/18th Royal Hussars
The Hawk, Regimental Journal of the 14th/20th King's Hussars
The Regimental Journal of 15th/19th The King's Royal Hussars
The Scarlet & Green Journal, Regimental Journal of the 16th/5th Queen's Royal Lancers

The Regimental Journal of the 17th/21st Lancers
Red Lanyard, The magazine of the First Royal Tank Regiment
Tank, The Royal Tank Regiment Journal

Langridge's Military Publications, 1958-60 Dress Distinctions of the:-

Queen's Bays (2nd Dragoon Guards)
3rd Carabiniers (POWDG)
4th/7th Royal Dragoon Guards
5th Royal Inniskilling Dragoon Guards
7th Queen's Own Hussars
Queen's Own Hussars
VIII King's Royal Irish Hussars
9th Queen's Royal Lancers
10th Royal Hussars
11th Hussars (PAO)
XII Royal Lancers
15th/19th King's Royal Hussars

Regiment magazine
No.9 – The King's Royal Hussars, 1715 – 1995
No.20 – The Queen's Royal Lancers, 1689 – 1997
No.26 – The Royal Tank Regiment, 1916 – 1997
No.34 – The Royal Dragoon Guards, 1685 – 1998

Arm Badges of the British Cavalry Regiments, Peter Seaman (Peter Seaman, 1994)
Badge Backings & Special Embellishments of the British Army (The Ulster Defence Regiment Benevolent Fund, 1992)
British Army Uniforms & Insignia of World War Two, Brian L Davis (Lionel Leventhal Ltd, 1983)
The British Army 1965 – 80, Major DG Smith (Osprey Publishing Ltd, 1977)
The British Army in the 1980s, Mike Chappell (Osprey Publishing Ltd, 1987)
British Army Badges, Lt-Col Robin Hodges (Lt-Col & Mrs R Hodges, 2005)
Cavalry Warrant Officers' and Non-Commissioned Officers' Arm Badges, David Linaker and Gordon Dine (The Military Historical Society, 1997)
Collecting Metal Shoulder Titles, RA Westlake (Frederick Warne, 1980)
Desert Rats, The British 4 and 7 Armoured Brigades, WWII to Today, Hans Halberstadt (Motorbooks International, 1993)
Flak Jackets, 20th Century Military Body Armour, Simon Dunstan (Osprey Publishing Ltd, 1984)
Head-dress Badges of the British Army, Volume Two: From the end of the Great War to the present day, Arthur L Kipling & Hugh L King (Muller, Bond & White, 1979)
The History of The 15th/19th The King's Royal Hussars, 1945-1980, Jeremy Bastin (Keats House Ltd, 1981)
Khaki Drill & Jungle Green, British Tropical Uniforms 1939-45 in colour photographs, Martin J Brayley & Richard Ingram (The Crowood Press, 2000)
Lineage Book of British Land Forces 1660 – 1978, JBM Frederick (Microform Academic Publishers, 1984)
The Medal Yearbook, 2006 (Token Publishing Ltd, 2006)
Military Badge Collecting, John Gaylor (Seeley, Service & Co, 1971)

The Regimental History of 1st The Queen's Dragoon Guards, Michael Mann (Queen's Dragoon Guards, 1993)
In the Finest Tradition, The Royal Scots Dragoon Guards (Carabiniers & Greys) Its History and Treasures, Stephen Wood (Mainstream Publishing Co (Edinburgh) Ltd, 1988)
The Ramnuggur Boys, 14th/20th King's Hussars 1715-1992, John Pharo-Tomlin (The Museum of the King's Royal Hussars in Lancashire, 2002)
Shot and Captured, photographs of the Royal Scots Dragoons Battlegroup in Iraq 2003, Tony Nicoletti and Major Aidan Stephen (Scottish Daily Record, 2003)
Uniforms of the Royal Armoured Corps, Malcolm Dawson (Almark Publishing Co Ltd, 1974)
.380 Enfield No.2 Revolver, Mark Stamps & Ian Skennerton (Ian D Skennerton, 1993)